Farm Girl Vi

by Lori Holt of Bee in my Bonnet

Farm Girl Vintage

Author and Designer - Lori Holt
Editor in Chief - Kimberly Jolly
Copy Editors - Cheryl Cohorn and Nova Birchfield
Art Director - Sarah Price
Photographers - Sarah Price and Jocelyn Ueng
Photographs taken in Austin, Texas, and Lori Holt's
quilty cottage in Riverton, Utah.

Other books by Lori Holt:

Lori Holt's blog: www.BeeInMyBonnetCo.blogspot.com

Published by:
Fat Quarter Shop®, PO Box 1544, Manchaca, Texas 78652
www.FatQuarterShop.com
www.ItsSewEmma.com

ISBN: 978-0-9881749-7-9

Table of Contents

Hmm ... which Farm Girl Quilt should I make first?

Introduction:

Farm Girl Blocks:

Barn & Tractor Blocks and Quilts:

Mix & Match Setting Quilts:

More Farm Girl Quilts:

About a Farm Girl

Before I was ever Bee in my Bonnet, I was a Farm Girl. Both of my parents grew up on farms as well as their parents, and their parents before them, and so on.

Our family's farm was a small one in Herriman, Utah, parceled out from land that was once part of the 10-acre orchard belonging to my maternal great-grandparents. In the nearby town of Bluffdale, Utah, my father's parents farmed their own 180 acres, so my brothers and sisters and I were raised with a deep, true rural heritage. Even now, I'm not more than a stone's throw away from my childhood home where my parents still live.

Life was good on the farm, and I lived a happy childhood growing up in the sunshine, surrounded by my grandparents, aunts, uncles and cousins. My parents taught me well. We went to church on Sundays, and the rest of the week we worked hard as a family to live on what we raised. I climbed trees, herded sheep, played in the garden, rode horses, drove tractors and spent plenty of time in the kitchen cooking and canning. And, of course, my mother taught me to sew.

This Farm Girl

Me and my three older sisters

In the pasture with our cow "Boss"

Carolyn, my mom, Debbie, my dad,
Brian, Tammy, Morgan and me

My family in our Sunday best

When it came to sewing, we made a lot of our own clothing and useful items for the kitchen, like aprons, dishtowels and potholders. Last, but not least, we made quilts! My grandparents lived by the old farmstead motto: "Use it up, wear it out, make it do or do without!" My mother taught me to make things that were not only useful but also pretty. After all, if these items were going to fill our home, why not also make them beautiful?

The seeds for the many quilts in my book grew from my childhood, and I can't wait to share them with you. We've got so much to do and just a few hours from sunrise to sunset, so let's plow on!

My grandparents on the farm

My grandma on the farm

My parents, Leon & Carol

My grandpa Crane

My dad

My grandparents at the herd

My mom with Aunt Doris and Uncle Lynn

My grandma Crane

My grandma and grandpa Ewell with Aunt ValLene

Before we get started, let me give you a quick lay of the land. This book is divided into four sections: Farm Girl Blocks, Barn & Tractor Blocks and Quilts, Mix & Match Setting Quilts and More Farm Girl Quilts.

Farm Girl Blocks

I've gathered 45 Farm Girl Blocks to use throughout my book. A few are traditional blocks with a new spin and a new name, but most are original designs drawn from my Farm Girl memories. There are instructions to make them in two sizes: 6" and 12". These blocks are a wonderful way to use up your fabric stash, and that is my preferred method of sewing. You will be amazed at how much scrap busting can be accomplished by making my Farm Girl Blocks!

If you've never worked with small pieces like the ones in my 6" quilt blocks, I advise you to shorten your stitch length and press all seams open. Yes, I said open! This will help flatten bulky seams and make it easier for block sections to line up accurately. For your 12" blocks, feel free to press your seams open or follow the pressing arrows provided in the block instructions. Also, be sure to save your larger easy corner triangle trimmings to use for smaller blocks later. Like my grandmother said, "Waste not, want not."

Try making one of my mini design boards to audition your fabrics and to lay out each block. It will quickly become an invaluable tool for your sewing. Instructions to make one are on my Bee in my Bonnet blog. I also like using Alphabitties

to label my fabrics. They lend a helping hand for working with lots of pieces and boost the cuteness factor. After all, even organization should be cute!

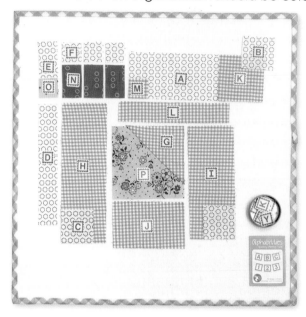

Barn & Tractor Blocks and Quilts

Barns and silos are essential parts of a farmstead, so these blocks and quilts are essential to my book!

Any of the 6" Farm Girl Blocks will fit snugly into the 14" Quilty Barn and Silo Barn Blocks, and I've topped them off with the cutest Tractor Block a Farm Girl could ever dream of.

Moving on to the quilts, I always say, **"You are the boss of your own quilt."** Select a medley of your favorite 6" Farm Girl Blocks to set into these barn and silo beauties to make these quilts your playground.

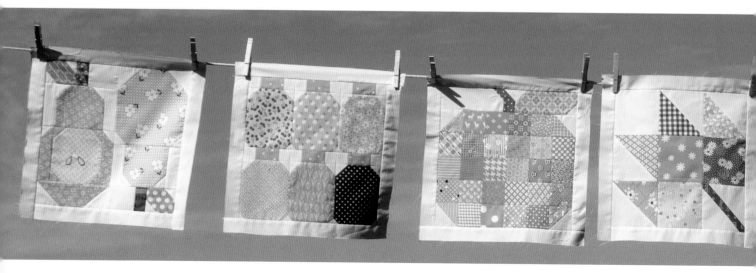

Mix & Match Setting Quilts

I have designed seven quilt settings for you to mix and match both the 6" and 12" blocks, and I encourage you to make all of these quilts, multiple times, with multiple Farm Girl Blocks!

Mixing and matching blocks with my quilt settings will be like making pies. If you choose one single block to savor, you will be blown away with the results. But don't limit yourself to just one flavor. Like a pie contest at the county fair, all pies are equally amazing and unique, just like your quilts will be.

No matter how many times you make these projects, a different block choice gives you a fresh new quilt. You have many to choose from so the possibilities are endless!

More Farm Girl Quilts

Sampler quilts make my quilty heart sing! Finishing one is a huge accomplishment. Assemble a multitude of Farm Girl Blocks into any of these three gorgeous projects. No two quilts will ever be the same, and they will all be made with love and care by your own two hands. That's all this Farm Girl could ever ask for!

How Will Your Garden Grow?

I've said it before, and I'll say it again, "You are the boss of your own quilt!" I want you to …

🐓 **Mix and match your blocks:**
With so many Farm Girl Blocks to choose from, don't limit yourself to the combinations I have included in this book. Imagine the Picnic Quilt Setting with Mama Hen and Baby Chick Blocks! The Sowing Seeds Tabletopper Setting is easy to change out for the holidays. Try my Winter Star Block for Christmas, my Egg Basket Block for Easter or my Old Glory Block for the 4th of July.

🐓 **Mix and match your fabrics:**
Pick colors to complement the mood of each quilt. In my Picnic Quilt Setting, bright reds, pinks and blues resonate with summer while yellows, oranges and greens whisper of autumn. Fabric styles and colors will shape your quilt's personality.

🐓 **Choose your block sizes:**
My County Fair Quilt Setting features a small and large version. With 6" blocks, you create an adorable mini quilt. With 12" blocks, the quilt is quite a vision! My Harvest Tablerunner Setting also offers two size options. Each is the same amount of cutting and sewing, so pick the one that suits your farm.

More than anything, I want you to love what you make. Make it usable, make it beautiful and make it the Farm Girl Vintage way!

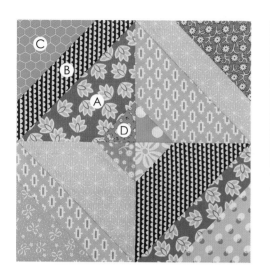

		6" Block	12" Block
Half Square Triangles *	A	2 - 3 ⅞" squares	2 - 6 ⅞" squares
Half Square Triangles *	B	2 - 3 ⅞" squares	2 - 6 ⅞" squares
Outer Triangles **	C	4 - 2 ½" squares	4 - 4 ½" squares
Inner Triangles **	D	4 - 1 ½" squares	4 - 2 ½" squares

* Use two different scrappy fabrics.
** Use four different scrappy fabrics.

Piecing Instructions:

Draw a diagonal line on the wrong side of the Fabric A squares.

With right sides facing, layer a Fabric A square with a Fabric B square.

Stitch ¼" from each side of the drawn line.

Cut apart on the marked line.

Half Square Triangle Unit should measure 3 ½" x 3 ½" (6 ½" x 6 ½").

Make four.

Make four.

Draw a diagonal line on the wrong side of the Fabric C squares.

With right sides facing, layer a Fabric C square on one corner of a Half Square Triangle Unit.

Follow diagrams for fabric placement.

Stitch on the drawn line and trim ¼" away from the seam.

Partial Apron Strings Unit should measure 3 ½" x 3 ½" (6 ½" x 6 ½").

Make four total.

Make one. Make one.
Make one. Make one.

Draw a diagonal line on the wrong side of the Fabric D squares.

With right sides facing, layer a Fabric D square on the opposite corner of a Partial Apron Strings Unit.

Follow diagrams for fabric placement.

Stitch on the drawn line and trim ¼" away from the seam.

Apron Strings Unit should measure 3 ½" x 3 ½" (6 ½" x 6 ½").

Make four total.

Make one. Make one.

Make one. Make one.

Assemble the Apron Strings Block.

Apron Strings Block should measure 6 ½" x 6 ½" (12 ½" x 12 ½").

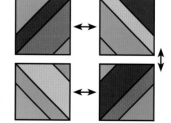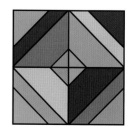

Autumn Star Block

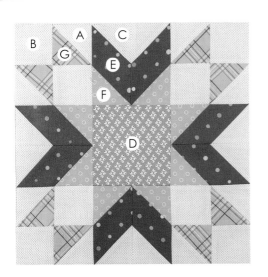

		6" Block	12" Block
Background	A	4 - 1 ⅞" squares	4 - 2 ⅞" squares
	B	8 - 1 ½" squares	8 - 2 ½" squares
	C	8 - 1 ½" squares	8 - 2 ½" squares
Center	D	1 - 2 ½" square	1 - 4 ½" square
Brown Star Points	E	8 - 1 ½" x 2 ½" rectangles	8 - 2 ½" x 4 ½" rectangles
Blue Star Points	F	8 - 1 ½" squares	8 - 2 ½" squares
Green Star Points	G	4 - 1 ⅞" squares	4 - 2 ⅞" squares

Piecing Instructions:

Draw a diagonal line on the wrong side of the Fabric C squares and the Fabric F squares.

With right sides facing, layer a Fabric C square on the top end of a Fabric E rectangle.

Stitch on the drawn line and trim ¼" away from the seam.

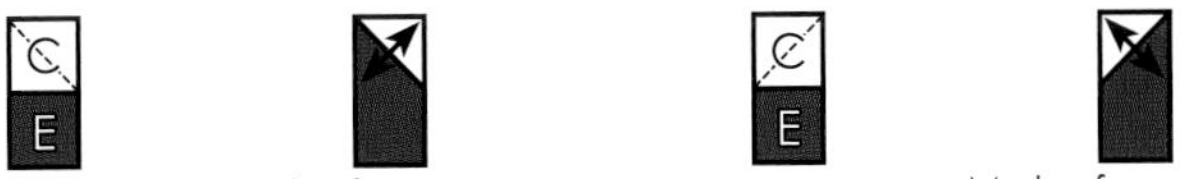

Make four
Left Star Units.

Make four
Right Star Units.

Repeat on the bottom end of the Fabric E rectangle with a Fabric F square.

Star Unit should measure 1 ½" x 2 ½" (2 ½" x 4 ½").

Make four Left Star Units. Make four Right Star Units. Make eight total.

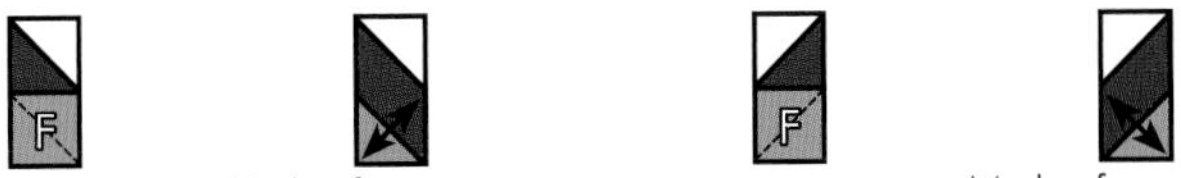

Make four
Left Star Units.

Make four
Right Star Units.

Assemble one Left Star Unit and one Right Star Unit.
Star Point Unit should measure 2 ½" x 2 ½" (4 ½" x 4 ½").
Make four.

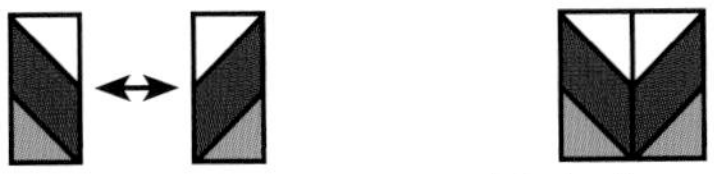

Make four.

Draw a diagonal line on the wrong side of the Fabric A squares.

With right sides facing, layer a Fabric A square with a Fabric G square.

Stitch ¼" from each side of the drawn line.

Cut apart on the marked line.

Half Square Triangle Unit should measure 1 ½" x 1 ½" (2 ½" x 2 ½").

Make eight.

Make eight.

Assemble two Fabric B squares and two Half Square Triangle Units.

Corner Unit should measure 2 ½" x 2 ½" (4 ½" x 4 ½").

Make four.

Make four.

Assemble the Autumn Star Block.

Autumn Star Block should measure 6 ½" x 6 ½" (12 ½" x 12 ½").

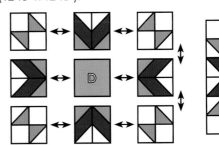

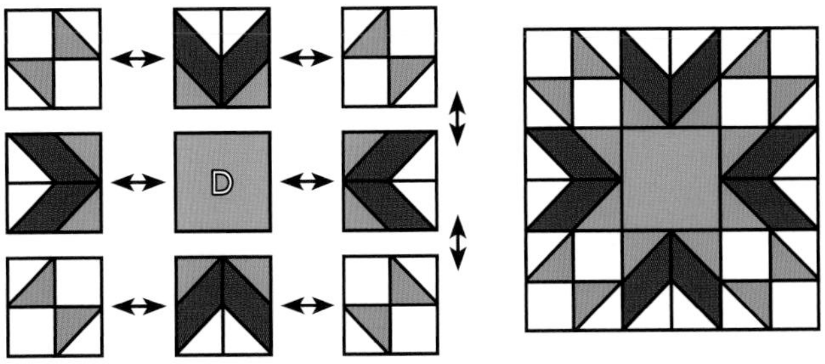

Baby Chick Block

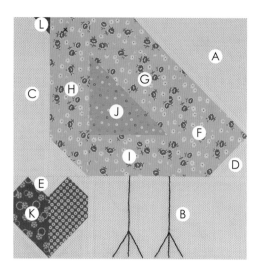

			6" Block	12" Block
Background	A	1 - 3 ½" square	1 - 6 ½" square
	B	1 - 2 ½" x 4 ½" rectangle	1 - 4 ½" x 8 ½" rectangle
	C	1 - 1 ½" x 4 ½" rectangle	1 - 2 ½" x 8 ½" rectangle
	D	4 - 1 ½" squares	4 - 2 ½" squares
	E	4 - 1" squares	4 - 1 ½" squares
Chick	F	1 - 2 ½" x 4 ½" rectangle	1 - 4 ½" x 8 ½" rectangle
	G	1 - 2 ½" square	1 - 4 ½" square
	H	1 - 1 ½" x 4 ½" rectangle	1 - 2 ½" x 8 ½" rectangle
	I	2 - 1 ½" x 2 ½" rectangles	2 - 2 ½" x 4 ½" rectangles
Wing	J	1 - 2 ½" square	1 - 4 ½" square
Heart *	K	2 - 1 ½" x 2 ½" rectangles	2 - 2 ½" x 4 ½" rectangles
Beak	L	1 - 1" square	1 - 1 ½" square

* Use two different scrappy fabrics.

Piecing Instructions:

Draw a diagonal line on the wrong side of the Fabric L square.

With right sides facing, layer the Fabric L square on the top right corner of the Fabric C rectangle.

Stitch on the drawn line and trim ¼" away from the seam.

Beak Unit should measure 1 ½" x 4 ½" (2 ½" x 8 ½").

Make one.

Make one.

Draw a diagonal line on the wrong side of the Fabric D squares.

With right sides facing, layer a Fabric D square on the bottom end of the Fabric H rectangle.

Stitch on the drawn line and trim ¼" away from the seam.

Left Baby Chick Unit should measure 1 ½" x 4 ½" (2 ½" x 8 ½").

Make one.

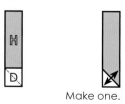

Make one.

Draw a diagonal line on the wrong side of the Fabric G square.

With right sides facing, layer the Fabric G square with the Fabric J square.

Stitch on the drawn line and trim ¼" away from the seam.

Wing Unit should measure 2 ½" x 2 ½" (4 ½" x 4 ½").

Make one.

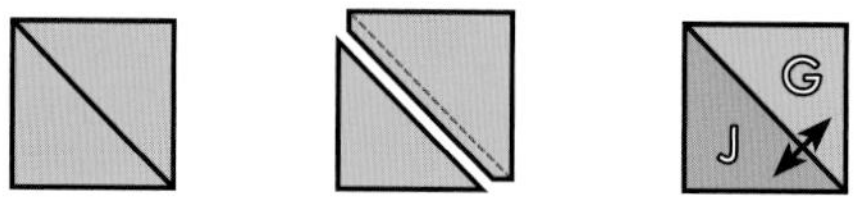

Make one.

Assemble two Fabric I rectangles and the Wing Unit.

Middle Baby Chick Unit should measure 2 ½" x 4 ½" (4 ½" x 8 ½").

Make one.

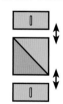 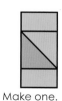

Make one.

With right sides facing, layer a Fabric D square on the bottom right corner of the Fabric F rectangle.

Stitch on the drawn line and trim ¼" away from the seam.

Right Baby Chick Unit should measure 2 ½" x 4 ½" (4 ½" x 8 ½").

Make one.

Make one.

Assemble the Beak Unit, the Left Baby Chick Unit, the Middle Baby Chick Unit and the Right Baby Chick Unit.

Partial Top Baby Chick Unit should measure 4 ½" x 6 ½" (8 ½" x 12 ½").

Make one.

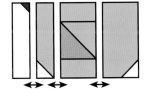

Make one.

Draw a diagonal line on the wrong side of the Fabric A square.

With right sides facing, layer the Fabric A square on the top right corner of the Partial Top Baby Chick Unit.

Stitch on the drawn line and trim ¼" away from the seam.

Top Baby Chick Unit should measure 4 ½" x 6 ½" (8 ½" x 12 ½").

Make one.

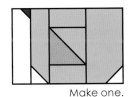

Make one.

Draw a diagonal line on the wrong side of the Fabric E squares.

With right sides facing, layer a Fabric E square on the top left corner of a Fabric K rectangle.

Stitch on the drawn line and trim ¼" away from the seam.

Make two.

Repeat on the top right corner of the Fabric K rectangle.

Partial Heart Unit should measure 1 ½" x 2 ½" (2 ½" x 4 ½").

Make two.

Make two.

With right sides facing, layer a Fabric D square on the bottom end of a Partial Heart Unit.

Stitch on the drawn line and trim ¼" away from the seam.

Pay close attention to unit placement.

Left Heart Unit should measure 1 ½" x 2 ½" (2 ½" x 4 ½").

Make one.

Make one.

With right sides facing, layer a Fabric D square on the bottom end of a Partial Heart Unit.

Stitch on the drawn line and trim ¼" away from the seam.

Pay close attention to unit placement.

Right Heart Unit should measure 1 ½" x 2 ½" (2 ½" x 4 ½").

Make one.

Make one.

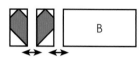
Assemble the Left Heart Unit, the Right Heart Unit and the Fabric B rectangle.

Bottom Baby Chick Unit should measure 2 ½" x 6 ½" (4 ½" x 12 ½").

Make one.

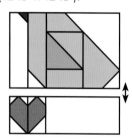
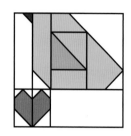

Make one.

Assemble the Baby Chick Block.

Baby Chick Block should measure 6 ½" x 6 ½" (12 ½" x 12 ½").

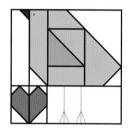

Embroider using three strands of embroidery floss and a backstitch.

6" Baby Chick Eye

6" Baby Chick Legs

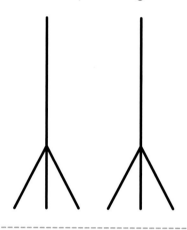

12" Baby Chick Eye

12" Baby Chick Legs

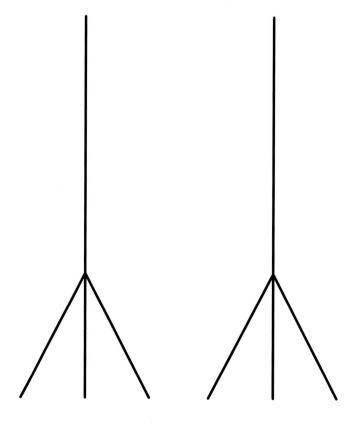

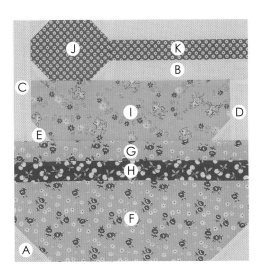

		6" Block	12" Block
Background	A	2 - 1 ½" squares	2 - 2 ½" squares
	B	2 - 1" x 4" rectangles	2 - 1 ½" x 7 ½" rectangles
	C	1 - 1" x 3 ½" rectangle	1 - 1 ½" x 6 ½" rectangle
	D	1 - 1" x 2" rectangle	1 - 1 ½" x 3 ½" rectangle
	E	6 - 1" squares	6 - 1 ½" squares
Large Bowl	F	1 - 2 ½" x 6 ½" rectangle	1 - 4 ½" x 12 ½" rectangle
	G	1 - 1" x 6 ½" rectangle	1 - 1 ½" x 12 ½" rectangle
Large Bowl Stripe	H	1 - 1" x 6 ½" rectangle	1 - 1 ½" x 12 ½" rectangle
Small Bowl	I	1 - 2" x 5 ½" rectangle	1 - 3 ½" x 10 ½" rectangle
Spoon	J	1 - 2" x 2 ½" rectangle	1 - 3 ½" x 4 ½" rectangle
	K	1 - 1" x 4" rectangle	1 - 1 ½" x 7 ½" rectangle

Piecing Instructions:

Draw a diagonal line on the wrong side of the Fabric E squares.

With right sides facing, layer a Fabric E square on one corner of the Fabric J rectangle.

Stitch on the drawn line and trim ¼" away from the seam.

Make one.

Repeat on the remaining corners of the Fabric J rectangle.

Spoon End Unit should measure 2" x 2 ½" (3 ½" x 4 ½").

Make one.

Make one.

Assemble two Fabric B rectangles and the Fabric K rectangle.

Spoon Handle Unit should measure 2" x 4" (3 ½" x 7 ½").

Make one.

Make one.

Assemble the Spoon End Unit and the Spoon Handle Unit.

Spoon Unit should measure 2" x 6" (3 ½" x 11 ½").

Make one.

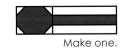 

Make one.

With right sides facing, layer a Fabric E square on the bottom left corner of the Fabric I rectangle.

Stitch on the drawn line and trim ¼" away from the seam.

Make one.

Repeat on the bottom right corner of the Fabric I rectangle.

Small Bowl Unit should measure 2" x 5 ½" (3 ½" x 10 ½").

Make one.

Make one.

Baking Day Block

Assemble the Small Bowl Unit and the Fabric D rectangle.

Spaced Small Bowl Unit should measure 2" x 6" (3 ½" x 11 ½").

Make one.

Make one.

Assemble the Spoon Unit and the Spaced Small Bowl Unit.

Spoon/Bowl Unit should measure 3 ½" x 6" (6 ½" x 11 ½").

Make one.

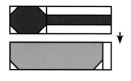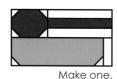

Make one.

Assemble the Fabric C rectangle and the Spoon/Bowl Unit.

Spaced Spoon/Bowl Unit should measure 3 ½" x 6 ½" (6 ½" x 12 ½").

Make one.

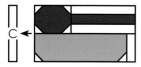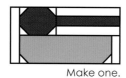

Make one.

Draw a diagonal line on the wrong side of the Fabric A squares.

With right sides facing, layer a Fabric A square on the bottom left corner of the Fabric F rectangle.

Stitch on the drawn line and trim ¼" away from the seam.

Make one.

Repeat on the bottom right corner of the Fabric F rectangle.

Bottom Large Bowl Unit should measure 2 ½" x 6 ½" (4 ½" x 12 ½").

Make one.

Make one.

Assemble the Fabric G rectangle, the Fabric H rectangle and the Bottom Large Bowl Unit.

Large Bowl Unit should measure 3 ½" x 6 ½" (6 ½" x 12 ½").

Make one.

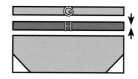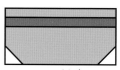

Make one.

Assemble the Baking Day Block.

Baking Day Block should measure 6 ½" x 6 ½" (12 ½" x 12 ½").

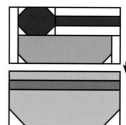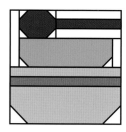

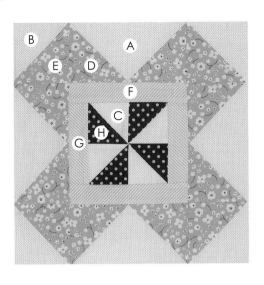

		6" Block	12" Block
Background	A	1 - 4 ¼" square	1 - 7 ¼" square
	B	2 - 2 ⅜" squares	2 - 3 ⅞" squares
	C	2 - 1 ⅞" squares	2 - 2 ⅞" squares
Outer Star	D	1 - 4 ¾" square	1 - 7 ¾" square
	E	2 - 2 ⅜" squares	2 - 3 ⅞" squares
Frame	F	2 - 1" x 3 ½" rectangles	2 - 1 ½" x 6 ½" rectangles
	G	2 - 1" x 2 ½" rectangles	2 - 1 ½" x 4 ½" rectangles
Pinwheel	H	2 - 1 ⅞" squares	2 - 2 ⅞" squares

Piecing Instructions:

Draw a diagonal line on the wrong side of the Fabric C squares.

With right sides facing, layer a Fabric C square with a Fabric H square.

Stitch ¼" from each side of the drawn line.

Cut apart on the marked line.

Small Half Square Triangle Unit should measure 1 ½" x 1 ½" (2 ½" x 2 ½").

Make four.

Make four.

Assemble four Small Half Square Triangle Units.

Pinwheel Unit should measure 2 ½" x 2 ½" (4 ½" x 4 ½").

Make one.

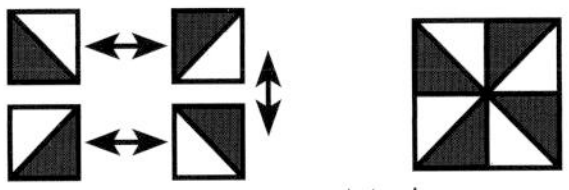

Make one.

Assemble two Fabric G rectangles, the Pinwheel Unit and two Fabric F rectangles.

Framed Pinwheel Unit should measure 3 ½" x 3 ½" (6 ½" x 6 ½").

Make one.

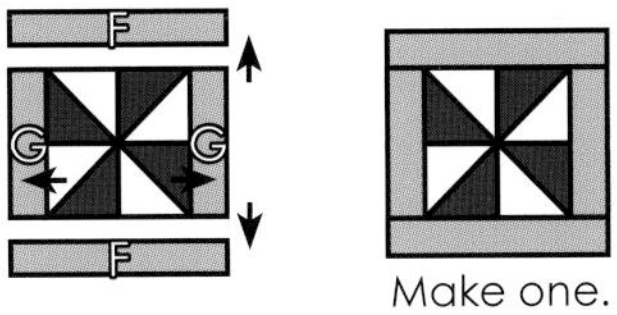

Make one.

Draw diagonal lines ¼" away from the center on the wrong side of the Fabric D square. Using a ½" x 6" ruler is helpful.

Make one.

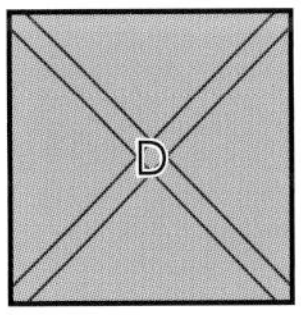

Make one.

Cut the Fabric D square into quarters.

Fabric D Unit should measure 2 ⅜" x 2 ⅜" (3 ⅞" x 3 ⅞").

Make four.

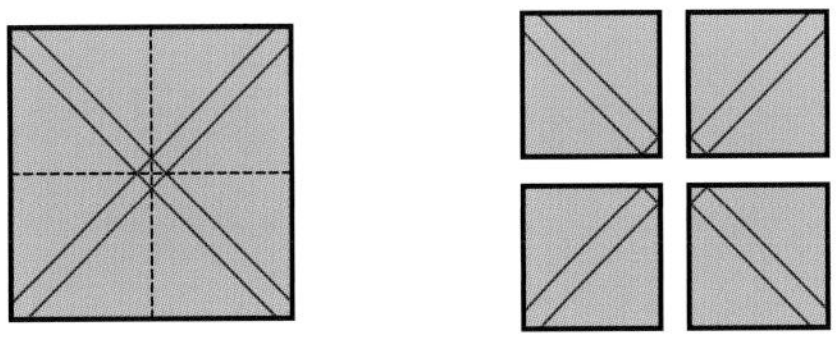

Make four.

Layer two Fabric D Units on opposite ends of the Fabric A square.

Stitch on the two drawn lines and cut apart between the stitched lines.

Make two.

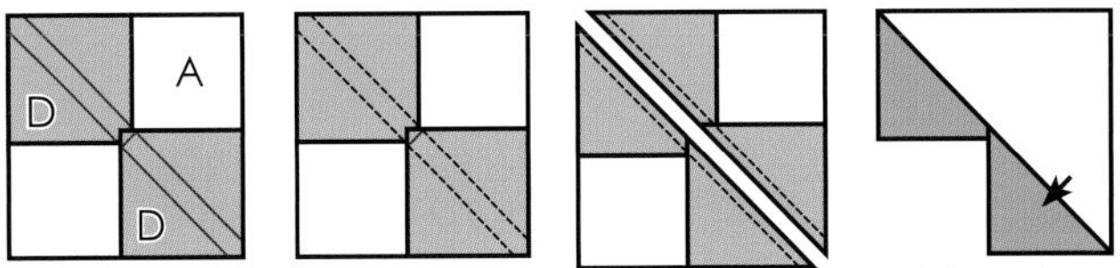

Make two.

Butter Churn Block

Layer one Fabric D Unit on the top right corner of a Fabric D/A Unit.

Stitch on the two drawn lines and cut apart between the stitched lines.

Flying Geese Unit should measure 2" x 3 ½" (3 ½" x 6 ½").

Make four.

Make four.

Draw a diagonal line on the wrong side of the Fabric B squares.

With right sides facing, layer a Fabric B square with a Fabric E square.

Stitch ¼" from each side of the drawn line.

Cut apart on the marked line.

Large Half Square Triangle Unit should measure 2" x 2" (3 ½" x 3 ½").

Make four.

Make four.

Assemble the Butter Churn Block.

Butter Churn Block should measure 6 ½" x 6 ½" (12 ½" x 12 ½").

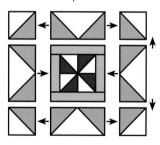 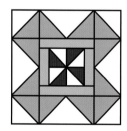

Canning Season Block

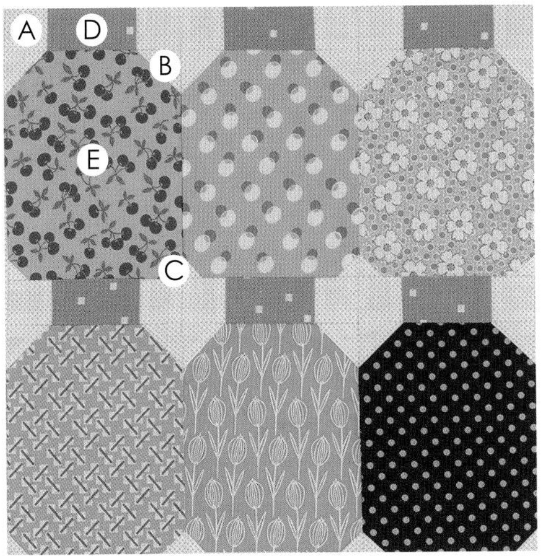

		6" Block	12" Block
Background	A	2 - 1" x 8" rectangles	2 - 1 ½" x 11" rectangles
	B	12 - 1" squares	12 - 1 ½" squares
	C	12 - ¾" squares	12 - 1" squares
Lids	D	1 - 1 ½" x 8" rectangle	1 - 2 ½" x 11" rectangle
Jars *	E	6 - 2 ½" x 3" rectangles	6 - 4 ½" x 5 ½" rectangles

** Use six different scrappy fabrics.*

Piecing Instructions:

Draw a diagonal line on the wrong side of the Fabric B squares and the Fabric C squares.

With right sides facing, layer two Fabric B squares on the top left and top right corners of a Fabric E rectangle.

Stitch on the drawn lines and trim ¼" away from the seam.

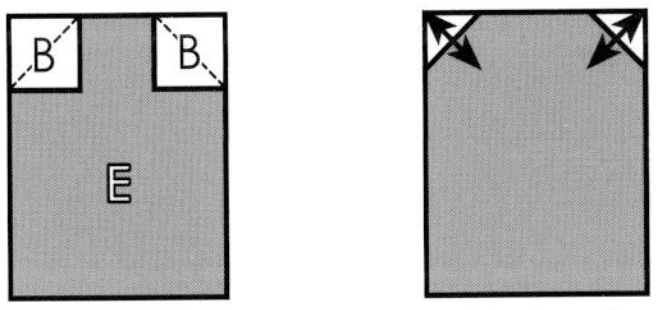

Make six.

Repeat on the bottom left and bottom right corners of the Fabric E rectangle with Fabric C squares.

Jar Unit should measure 2 ½" x 3" (4 ½" x 5 ½").

Make six.

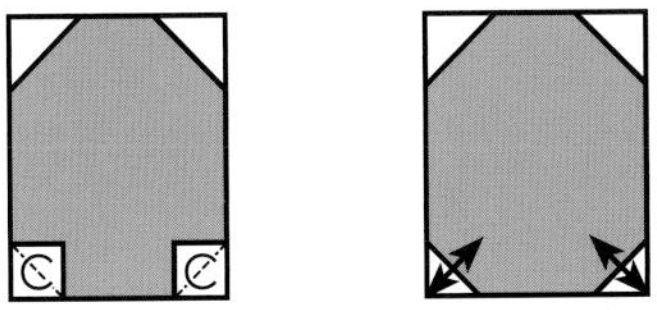

Make six.

Assemble two Fabric A rectangles and the Fabric D rectangle.

Lid Strip Unit should measure 2 ½" x 8" (4 ½" x 11").

Make one.

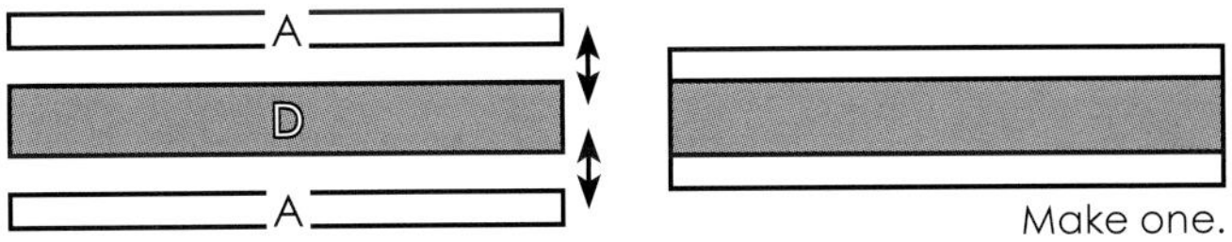

Make one.

Subcut the Lid Strip Unit into six 1" x 2 ½" (1 ½" x 4 ½") rectangles.

Lid Unit should measure 1" x 2 ½" (1 ½" x 4 ½").

Make six.

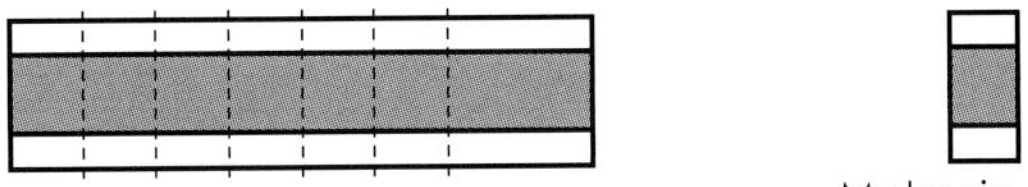

Make six.

Assemble the Canning Season Block.

Canning Season Block should measure 6 ½" x 6 ½" (12 ½" x 12 ½").

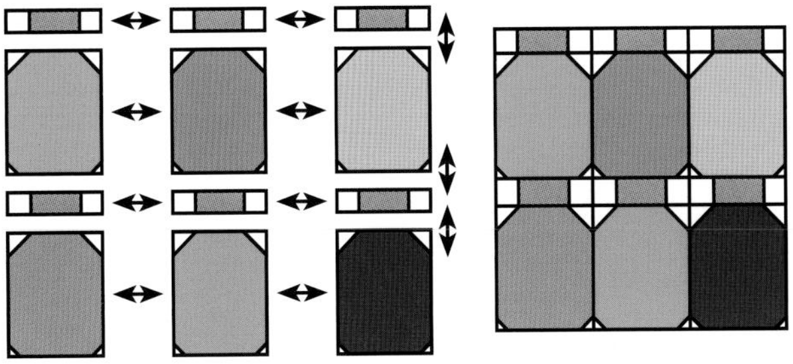

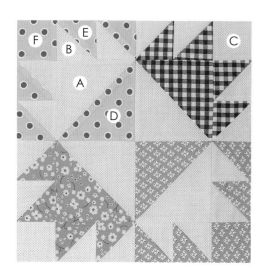

		6" Block	12" Block
Background	A	4 - 2 ½" squares	4 - 4 ½" squares
	B	16 - 1 ½" squares	16 - 2 ½" squares
	C	2 - 1 ½" squares	2 - 2 ½" squares
Chicken Feet *	D	4 - 2 ½" squares	4 - 4 ½" squares
	E	16 - 1 ½" squares	16 - 2 ½" squares
	F	2 - 1 ½" squares	2 - 2 ½" squares

* Use four different scrappy fabrics.

Piecing Instructions:

Draw a diagonal line on the wrong side of the Fabric A squares.

With right sides facing, layer a Fabric A square with a Fabric D square.

Stitch on the drawn line and trim ¼" away from the seam.

Large Half Square Triangle Unit should measure 2 ½" x 2 ½" (4 ½" x 4 ½").

Make four.

Make four.

Draw a diagonal line on the wrong side of the Fabric B squares.

With right sides facing, layer a Fabric B square with a Fabric E square.

Stitch on the drawn line and trim ¼" away from the seam.

Small Half Square Triangle Unit should measure 1 ½" x 1 ½" (2 ½" x 2 ½").

Make sixteen.

Make sixteen.

Assemble one Background Chicken Foot Unit.

Background Chicken Foot Unit should measure 3 ½" x 3 ½" (6 ½" x 6 ½").

Make two.

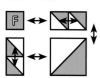

Make two.

Assemble one Print Chicken Foot Unit.

Print Chicken Foot Unit should measure 3 ½" x 3 ½" (6 ½" x 6 ½").

Make two.

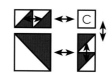

Make two.

Assemble the Chicken Foot Block.

Chicken Foot Block should measure 6 ½" x 6 ½" (12 ½" x 12 ½").

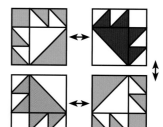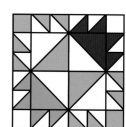

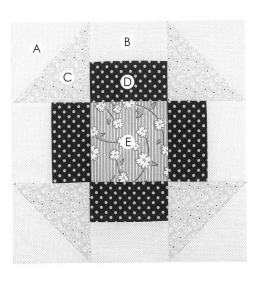

		6" Block	12" Block
Background	A	4 - 2 ½" squares	4 - 4 ½" squares
	B	4 - 1 ½" x 2 ½" rectangles	4 - 2 ½" x 4 ½" rectangles
Half Square Triangles	C	4 - 2 ½" squares	4 - 4 ½" squares
Ring	D	4 - 1 ½" x 2 ½" rectangles	4 - 2 ½" x 4 ½" rectangles
Center	E	1 - 2 ½" square	1 - 4 ½" square

Piecing Instructions:

Draw a diagonal line on the wrong side of the Fabric A squares.

With right sides facing, layer a Fabric A square with a Fabric C square.

Stitch on the drawn line and trim ¼" away from the seam.

Half Square Triangle Unit should measure 2 ½" x 2 ½" (4 ½" x 4 ½").

Make four.

Make four.

Assemble one Fabric B rectangle and one Fabric D rectangle.

Ring Unit should measure 2 ½" x 2 ½" (4 ½" x 4 ½").

Make four.

Make four.

Assemble the Churn Dash Block.

Churn Dash Block should measure 6 ½" x 6 ½" (12 ½" x 12 ½").

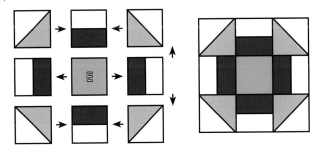

Cool Threads Block

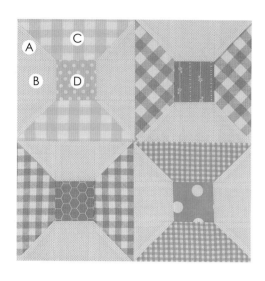

		6" Block	12" Block
Background	A	16 - 1 ½" squares	16 - 2 ½" squares
	B	8 - 1 ½" squares	8 - 2 ½" squares
Spools *	C	8 - 1 ½" x 3 ½" rectangles	8 - 2 ½" x 6 ½" rectangles
Thread *	D	4 - 1 ½" squares	4 - 2 ½" squares

* Use four different scrappy fabrics.

Piecing Instructions:

Draw a diagonal line on the wrong side of the Fabric A squares.

With right sides facing, layer a Fabric A square on one end of a Fabric C rectangle.

Stitch on the drawn line and trim ¼" away from the seam.

Make eight.

Repeat on the opposite end of the Fabric C rectangle.

Spool End Unit should measure 1 ½" x 3 ½" (2 ½" x 6 ½").

Make eight.

Make eight.

Assemble two Fabric B squares and one Fabric D square.

Thread Unit should measure 1 ½" x 3 ½" (2 ½" x 6 ½").

Make four.

Make four.

Assemble two matching Spool End Units and one coordinating Thread Unit.

Cool Threads Unit should measure 3 ½" x 3 ½" (6 ½" x 6 ½").

Make four.

Make four.

Assemble the Cool Threads Block.

Cool Threads Block should measure 6 ½" x 6 ½" (12 ½" x 12 ½").

 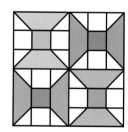

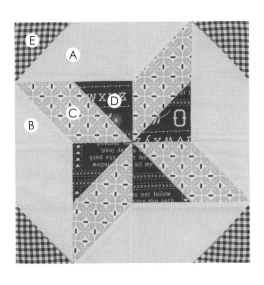

		6" Block	12" Block
Background	A	4 - 2" x 3 ½" rectangles	4 - 3 ½" x 6 ½" rectangles
	B	4 - 2" squares	4 - 3 ½" squares
Corn	C	4 - 2" x 3 ½" rectangles	4 - 3 ½" x 6 ½" rectangles
Tomatoes	D	4 - 2" squares	4 - 3 ½" squares
Corners	E	4 - 2" squares	4 - 3 ½" squares

Piecing Instructions:

Draw a diagonal line on the wrong side of the Fabric E squares.

With right sides facing, layer a Fabric E square on the left end of a Fabric A rectangle.

Stitch on the drawn line and trim ¼" away from the seam.

Corner Unit should measure 2" x 3 ½" (3 ½" x 6 ½").

Make four.

Make four.

Draw a diagonal line on the wrong side of the Fabric B squares and the Fabric D squares.

With right sides facing, layer a Fabric B square on the left end of a Fabric C rectangle.

Stitch on the drawn line and trim ¼" away from the seam.

Make four.

Repeat on the right end of the Fabric C rectangle with a Fabric D square.

Diagonal Unit should measure 2" x 3 ½" (3 ½" x 6 ½").

Make four.

Make four.

Assemble one Corner Unit and one Diagonal Unit.

Corn and Tomatoes Unit should measure 3 ½" x 3 ½" (6 ½" x 6 ½").

Make four.

Make four.

Assemble the Corn and Tomatoes Block.

Corn and Tomatoes Block should measure 6 ½" x 6 ½" (12 ½" x 12 ½").

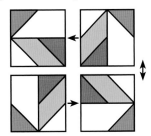 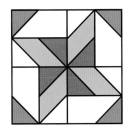

Country Crossroads Block

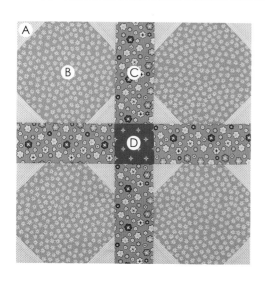

		6" Block	12" Block
Background	A	16 - 1 ¼" squares	16 - 2" squares
Snowballs	B	4 - 3" squares	4 - 5 ½" squares
Sashing	C	4 - 1 ½" x 3" rectangles	4 - 2 ½" x 5 ½" rectangles
Center	D	1 - 1 ½" square	1 - 2 ½" square

Piecing Instructions:

Draw a diagonal line on the wrong side of the Fabric A squares.

With right sides facing, layer a Fabric A square on one corner of a Fabric B square.

Stitch on the drawn line and trim ¼" away from the seam.

Make four.

Repeat on the remaining corners of the Fabric B square.

Snowball Unit should measure 3" x 3" (5 ½" x 5 ½).

Make four.

Make four.

Assemble the Country Crossroads Block.

Country Crossroads Block should measure 6 ½" x 6 ½" (12 ½" x 12 ½").

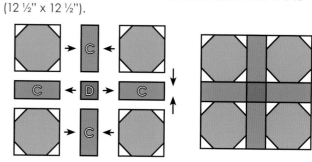

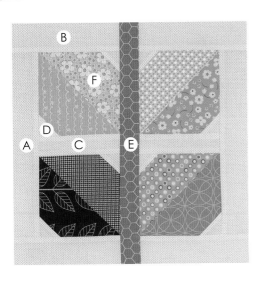

			6" Block	12" Block
Background	A	2 - 1 ¼" x 5" rectangles	2 - 2" x 9 ½" rectangles	
	B	4 - 1 ¼" x 3 ¼" rectangles	4 - 2" x 6" rectangles	
	C	2 - 1" x 2 ½" rectangles	2 - 1 ½" x 4 ½" rectangles	
	D	8 - 1" squares	8 - 1 ½" squares	
Stem	E	1 - 1" x 6 ½" rectangle	1 - 1 ½" x 12 ½" rectangle	
Leaves *	F	8 - 2 ½" squares	8 - 4 ½" squares	

* Use eight different scrappy fabrics.

Piecing Instructions:

Draw a diagonal line on the wrong side of four of the Fabric F squares.

With right sides facing, layer two coordinating Fabric F squares.

Stitch on the drawn line and trim ¼" away from the seam.

Half Square Triangle Unit should measure 2 ½" x 2 ½" (4 ½" x 4 ½").

Make four.

Make four.

Draw a diagonal line on the wrong side of the Fabric D squares.

With right sides facing, layer a Fabric D square on the top right corner of a Half Square Triangle Unit.

Stitch on the drawn line and trim ¼" away from the seam.

Make four.

Repeat on the bottom left corner of the Half Square Triangle Unit.

Leaf Unit should measure 2 ½" x 2 ½" (4 ½" x 4 ½").

Make four.

Make four.

Assemble two Leaf Units, one Fabric C rectangle and one Fabric A rectangle.

Left Crops Unit should measure 3 ¼" x 5" (6" x 9 ½").

Make one.

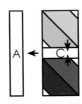

Make one.

Assemble two Leaf Units, one Fabric C rectangle and one Fabric A rectangle.

Right Crops Unit should measure 3 ¼" x 5" (6" x 9 ½").

Make one.

Make one.

Assemble the Crops Block.

Crops Block should measure 6 ½" x 6 ½" (12 ½" x 12 ½").

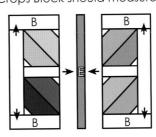 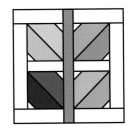

Egg Basket Block

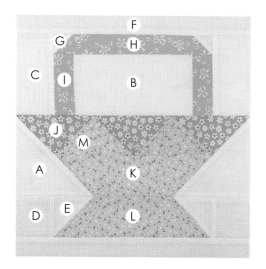

		6" Block	12" Block
Background	A	2 - 2 ½" squares	2 - 4 ½" squares
	B	1 - 2" x 3 ½" rectangle	1 - 3 ½" x 6 ½" rectangle
	C	2 - 1 ½" x 2 ½" rectangles	2 - 2 ½" x 4 ½" rectangles
	D	2 - 1 ½" squares	2 - 2 ½" squares
	E	2 - 1 ½" squares	2 - 2 ½" squares
	F	2 - 1" x 6 ½" rectangles	2 - 1 ½" x 12 ½" rectangles
	G	2 - 1" squares	2 - 1 ½" squares
Handle	H	1 - 1" x 4 ½" rectangle	1 - 1 ½" x 8 ½" rectangle
	I	2 - 1" x 2" rectangles	2 - 1 ½" x 3 ½" rectangles
Trim	J	3 - 1 ½" x 2 ½" rectangles	3 - 2 ½" x 4 ½" rectangles
Basket	K	1 - 1 ½" x 6 ½" rectangle	1 - 2 ½" x 12 ½" rectangle
	L	1 - 1 ½" x 4 ½" rectangle	1 - 2 ½" x 8 ½" rectangle
	M	4 - 1 ½" squares	4 - 2 ½" squares

Piecing Instructions:

Draw a diagonal line on the wrong side of the Fabric G squares.

With right sides facing, layer a Fabric G square on one end of the Fabric H rectangle.

Stitch on the drawn line and trim ¼" away from the seam.

Repeat on the opposite end of the Fabric H rectangle.

Handle Top Unit should measure 1" x 4 ½" (1 ½" x 8 ½").

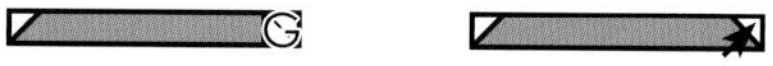

Make one.

Assemble two Fabric I rectangles and the Fabric B rectangle.

Handle Bottom Unit should measure 2" x 4 ½" (3 ½" x 8 ½").

Make one.

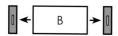

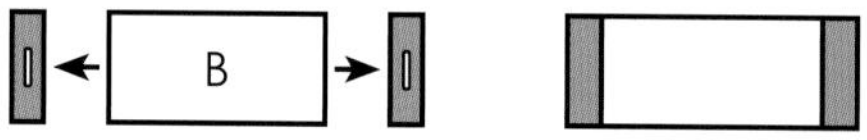

Make one.

Assemble the Handle Top Unit, the Handle Bottom Unit and two Fabric C rectangles.

Handle Unit should measure 2 ½" x 6 ½" (4 ½" x 12 ½").

Make one.

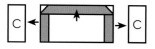 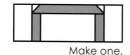

Make one.

Draw a diagonal line on the wrong side of the Fabric M squares.

With right sides facing, layer a Fabric M square on the right end of a Fabric J rectangle.

Stitch on the drawn line and trim ¼" away from the seam.

Left Trim Unit should measure 1 ½" x 2 ½" (2 ½" x 4 ½").

Make one.

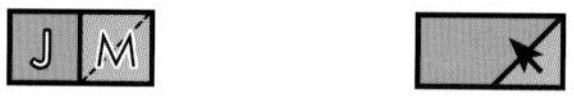

Make one.

With right sides facing, layer a Fabric M square on one end of a Fabric J rectangle.

Stitch on the drawn line and trim ¼" away from the seam.

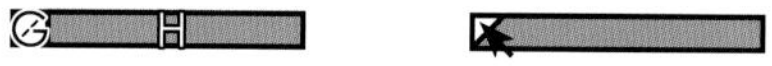

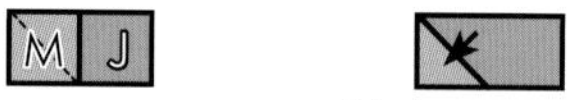

Make one.

Repeat on the opposite end of the Fabric J rectangle.

Center Trim Unit should measure 1 ½" x 2 ½" (2 ½" x 4 ½").

Make one.

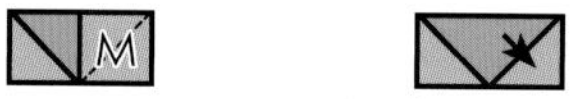

Make one.

With right sides facing, layer a Fabric M square on the left end of a Fabric J rectangle.

Stitch on the drawn line and trim ¼" away from the seam.

Right Trim Unit should measure 1 ½" x 2 ½" (2 ½" x 4 ½").

Make one.

Make one.

Assemble the Left Trim Unit, the Center Trim Unit and the Right Trim Unit.

Trim Unit should measure 1 ½" x 6 ½" (2 ½" x 12 ½").

Make one.

Make one.

Assemble the Trim Unit and the Fabric K rectangle.

Partial Basket Body Unit should measure 2 ½" x 6 ½" (4 ½" x 12 ½").

Make one.

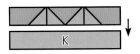

Make one.

Draw a diagonal line on the wrong side of the Fabric A squares.

With right sides facing, layer a Fabric A square on one end of the Partial Basket Body Unit.

Stitch on the drawn line and trim ¼" away from the seam.

Make one.

Repeat on the opposite end of the Partial Basket Body Unit.

Basket Body Unit should measure 2 ½" x 6 ½" (4 ½" x 12 ½").

Make one.

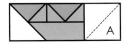

Make one.

Draw a diagonal line on the wrong side of the Fabric E squares.

With right sides facing, layer a Fabric E square on one end of the Fabric L rectangle.

Stitch on the drawn line and trim ¼" away from the seam.

Make one.

Repeat on the opposite end of the Fabric L rectangle.

Partial Basket Base Unit should measure 1 ½" x 4 ½" (2 ½" x 8 ½").

Make one.

Make one.

Assemble two Fabric D squares and the Partial Basket Base Unit.

Basket Base Unit should measure 1 ½" x 6 ½" (2 ½" x 12 ½").

Make one.

Make one.

Assemble the Egg Basket Block.

Egg Basket Block should measure 6 ½" x 6 ½" (12 ½" x 12 ½").

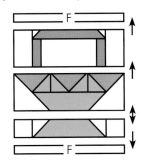 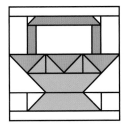

Farm Fresh Flower Block

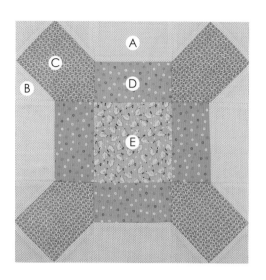

		6" Block	12" Block
Background	A	4 - 1 ½" x 2 ½" rectangles	4 - 2 ½" x 4 ½" rectangles
	B	12 - 1 ½" squares	12 - 2 ½" squares
Corners	C	4 - 2 ½" squares	4 - 4 ½" squares
Ring	D	4 - 1 ½" x 2 ½" rectangles	4 - 2 ½" x 4 ½" rectangles
Center	E	1 - 2 ½" square	1 - 4 ½" square

Piecing Instructions:

Draw a diagonal line on the wrong side of the Fabric B squares.

With right sides facing, layer two Fabric B squares on the top right and bottom left corners of a Fabric C square.

Stitch on the drawn lines and trim ¼" away from the seam.

Make four.

Repeat on the top left corner of the Fabric C square.

Corner Unit should measure 2 ½" x 2 ½" (4 ½" x 4 ½").

Make four.

Make four.

Assemble one Fabric A rectangle and one Fabric D rectangle.

Ring Unit should measure 2 ½" x 2 ½" (4 ½" x 4 ½").

Make four.

Make four.

Assemble the Farm Fresh Flower Block.

Farm Fresh Flower Block should measure 6 ½" x 6 ½" (12 ½" x 12 ½").

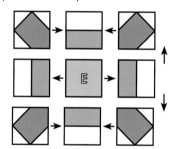 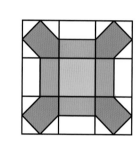

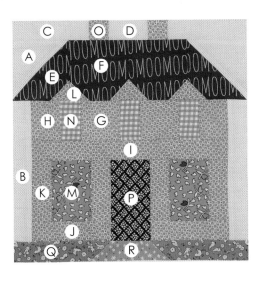

		6" Block	12" Block
Background	A	1 - 2 ⅜" square	1 - 3 ⅞" square
	B	2 - 1" x 4" rectangles	2 - 1 ½" x 7 ½" rectangles
	C	2 - 1" x 2 ½" rectangles	2 - 1 ½" x 4 ½" rectangles
	D	1 - 1" x 1 ½" rectangle	1 - 1 ½" x 2 ½" rectangle
Roof	E	1 - 2 ⅜" square	1 - 3 ⅞" square
	F	2 - 2" squares	2 - 3 ½" squares
House	G	2 - 1 ½" squares	2 - 2 ½" squares
	H	2 - 1 ¼" x 1 ½" rectangles	2 - 2" x 2 ½" rectangles
	I	1 - 1" x 5 ½" rectangle	1 - 1 ½" x 10 ½" rectangle
	J	2 - 1" x 2 ½" rectangles	2 - 1 ½" x 4 ½" rectangles
	K	4 - 1" x 2" rectangles	4 - 1 ½" x 3 ½" rectangles
	L	6 - 1" squares	6 - 1 ½" squares
Lower Windows	M	2 - 1 ½" x 2" rectangles	2 - 2 ½" x 3 ½" rectangles
Upper Windows	N	3 - 1" x 1 ½" rectangles	3 - 1 ½" x 2 ½" rectangles
Chimneys	O	2 - 1" squares	2 - 1 ½" squares
Door	P	1 - 1 ½" x 2 ½" rectangle	1 - 2 ½" x 4 ½" rectangle
Grass	Q	2 - 1" x 3" rectangles	2 - 1 ½" x 5 ½" rectangles
Sidewalk	R	1 - 1" x 2 ½" rectangle	1 - 1 ½" x 4 ½" rectangle

Piecing Instructions:

Assemble two Fabric C rectangles, two Fabric O squares and the Fabric D rectangle.

Chimney Unit should measure 1" x 6 ½" (1 ½" x 12 ½").

Make one.

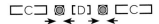 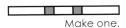

Make one.

Draw a diagonal line on the wrong side of the Fabric A square.

With right sides facing, layer the Fabric A square with the Fabric E square.

Stitch ¼" from each side of the drawn line.

Cut apart on the marked line.

Half Square Triangle Unit should measure 2" x 2" (3 ½" x 3 ½").

Make two.

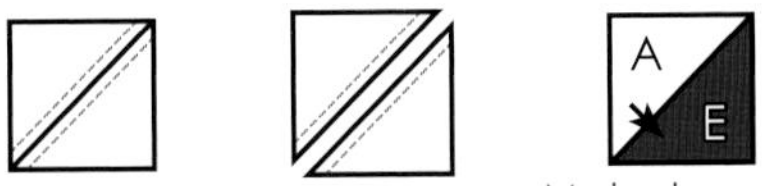

Make two.

Draw a diagonal line on the wrong side of the Fabric L squares.

With right sides facing, layer a Fabric L square on the bottom right corner of a Half Square Triangle Unit.

Pay close attention to unit placement.

Stitch on the drawn line and trim ¼" away from the seam.

Side Roof Unit should measure 2" x 2" (3 ½" x 3 ½").

Make two.

Make two.

With right sides facing, layer a Fabric L square on the bottom left corner of a Fabric F square.

Stitch on the drawn line and trim ¼" away from the seam.

Make two.

Repeat on the bottom right corner of the Fabric F square.

Middle Roof Unit should measure 2" x 2" (3 ½" x 3 ½").

Make two.

Make two.

Assemble two Side Roof Units and two Middle Roof Units.

Roof Unit should measure 2" x 6 ½" (3 ½" x 12 ½").

Make one.

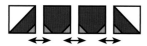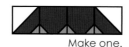

Make one.

Assemble two Fabric H rectangles, three Fabric N rectangles and two Fabric G squares.

Upper Window Unit should measure 1 ½" x 5 ½" (2 ½" x 10 ½").

Make one.

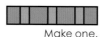

Make one.

Assemble two Fabric K rectangles and one Fabric M rectangle.

Lower Window Unit should measure 2" x 2 ½" (3 ½" x 4 ½").

Make two.

Make two.

Assemble one Lower Window Unit and one Fabric J rectangle.

Window Unit should measure 2 ½" x 2 ½" (4 ½" x 4 ½").

Make two.

Make two.

Assemble two Window Units and the Fabric P rectangle.

Bottom House Unit should measure 2 ½" x 5 ½" (4 ½" x 10 ½").

Make one.

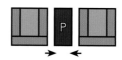

Make one.

Assemble the Upper Window Unit, the Fabric I rectangle, the Bottom House Unit and two Fabric B rectangles.

House Unit should measure 4" x 6 ½" (7 ½" x 12 ½").

Make one.

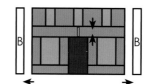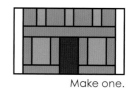

Make one.

On the wrong side of the Fabric R rectangle, mark a dot 1" (1 ½") up from the bottom right corner.

Draw a line from the bottom left corner to the dot.

With right sides facing, layer the marked Fabric R rectangle with a Fabric Q rectangle.

Stitch on the drawn line and trim ¼" away from the seam.

Partial Grass Unit should measure 1" x 4 ½" (1 ½" x 8 ½").

Make one.

Make one.

- -

On the wrong side of the remaining Fabric Q rectangle, mark a dot 1" (1 ½") down from the top right corner.

Draw a line from the top left corner to the dot.

With right sides facing, layer the marked Fabric Q rectangle with the Partial Grass Unit.

Stitch on the drawn line and trim ¼" away from the seam.

Grass Unit should measure 1" x 6 ½" (1 ½" x 12 ½").

Make one.

Make one.

Assemble the Farmhouse Block.

Farmhouse Block should measure 6 ½" x 6 ½" (12 ½" x 12 ½").

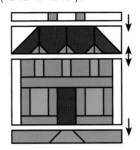 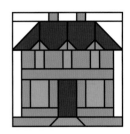

Feed and Seed Block

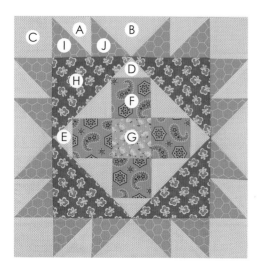

		6" Block	12" Block
Background	A	4 - 1 ⅞" squares	4 - 2 ⅞" squares
	B	4 - 1 ½" x 2 ½" rectangles	4 - 2 ½" x 4 ½" rectangles
	C	8 - 1 ½" squares	8 - 2 ½" squares
	D	2 - 1" x 4 ½" rectangles	2 - 1 ½" x 8 ½" rectangles
	E	2 - 1" x 3 ½" rectangles	2 - 1 ½" x 6 ½" rectangles
Cross Points	F	4 - 1 ½" squares	4 - 2 ½" squares
Cross Center	G	1 - 1 ½" square	1 - 2 ½" square
Triangles	H	4 - 2 ½" squares	4 - 4 ½" squares
Star Points	I	4 - 1 ⅞" squares	4 - 2 ⅞" squares
	J	8 - 1 ½" squares	8 - 2 ½" squares

Piecing Instructions:

Draw a diagonal line on the wrong side of the Fabric A squares.

With right sides facing, layer a Fabric A square with a Fabric I square.

Stitch ¼" from each side of the drawn line.

Cut apart on the marked line.

Half Square Triangle Unit should measure 1 ½" x 1 ½" (2 ½" x 2 ½").

Make eight.

Make eight.

Draw a diagonal line on the wrong side of the Fabric J squares.

With right sides facing, layer a Fabric J square on one end of a Fabric B rectangle.

Stitch on the drawn line and trim ¼" away from the seam.

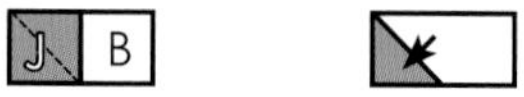

Make four.

Repeat on the opposite end of the Fabric B rectangle.

Flying Geese Unit should measure 1 ½" x 2 ½" (2 ½" x 4 ½").

Make four.

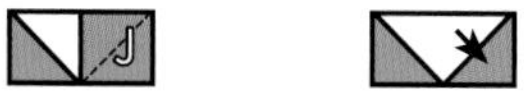

Make four.

Assemble two Half Square Triangle Units and one Flying Geese Unit.

Star Point Unit should measure 1 ½" x 4 ½" (2 ½" x 8 ½").

Make four.

Make four.

Assemble four Fabric C squares, four Fabric F squares and the Fabric G square.

Nine Patch Unit should measure 3 ½" x 3 ½" (6 ½" x 6 ½").

Make one.

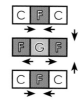

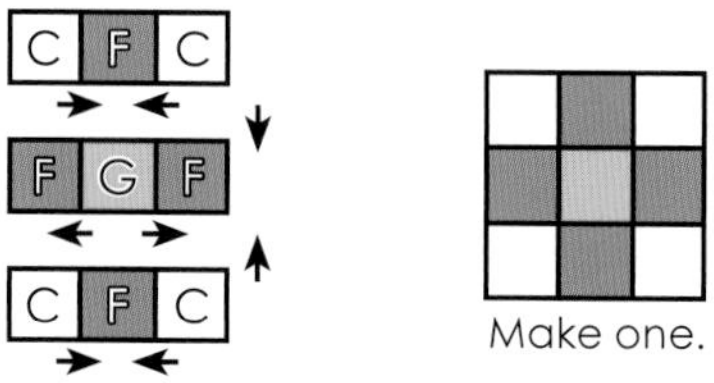

Make one.

Assemble two Fabric E rectangles, the Nine Patch Unit and two Fabric D rectangles.

Framed Nine Patch Unit should measure 4 ½" x 4 ½" (8 ½" x 8 ½").

Make one.

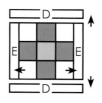

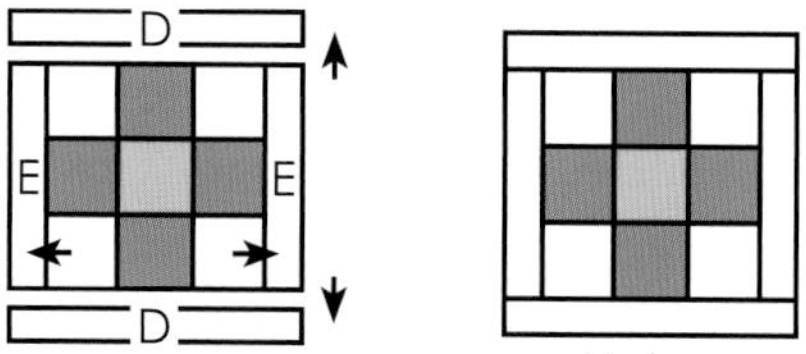

Make one.

Draw a diagonal line on the wrong side of the Fabric H squares.

With right sides facing, layer two Fabric H squares on opposite corners of the Framed Nine Patch Unit.

Stitch on the drawn lines and trim ¼" away from the seam.

Make one.

Repeat on the remaining corners of the Framed Nine Patch Unit.

Center Unit should measure 4 ½" x 4 ½" (8 ½" x 8 ½").

Make one.

Make one.

Assemble the Feed and Seed Block.

Feed and Seed Block should measure 6 ½" x 6 ½" (12 ½" x 12 ½").

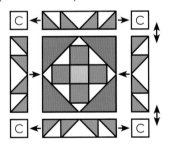 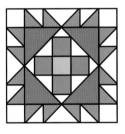

Fresh Pears Block

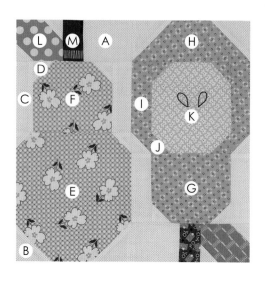

		6" Block	12" Block
Background	A	2 - 1 ½" x 1 ¾" rectangles	2 - 2 ½" x 3" rectangles
	B	4 - 1 ½" squares	4 - 2 ½" squares
	C	4 - 1" x 2 ¼" rectangles	4 - 1 ½" x 4" rectangles
	D	12 - 1" squares	12 - 1 ½" squares
Left Pear	E	1 - 3 ½" x 3 ¾" rectangle	1 - 6 ½" x 7" rectangle
	F	1 - 2 ¼" x 2 ½" rectangle	1 - 4" x 4 ½" rectangle
Right Pear Outside	G	1 - 2 ¼" x 2 ½" rectangle	1 - 4" x 4 ½" rectangle
	H	1 - 1 ½" x 3 ½" rectangle	1 - 2 ½" x 6 ½" rectangle
	I	2 - 1" x 2 ¾" rectangles	2 - 1 ½" x 5" rectangles
	J	4 - 1" squares	4 - 1 ½" squares
Right Pear Inside	K	1 - 2 ½" x 2 ¾" rectangle	1 - 4 ½" x 5" rectangle
Leaves *	L	2 - 1 ½" x 1 ¾" rectangles	2 - 2 ½" x 3" rectangles
Stems *	M	2 - 1" x 1 ½" rectangles	2 - 1 ½" x 2 ½" rectangles

Use two different scrappy fabrics.

Piecing Instructions:

Draw a diagonal line on the wrong side of the Fabric D squares.

With right sides facing, layer a Fabric D square on the top right corner of a Fabric L rectangle.

Stitch on the drawn line and trim ¼" away from the seam.

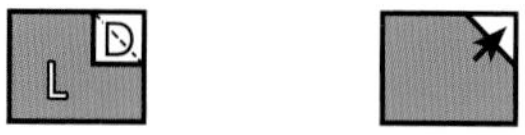

Make two.

Repeat on the bottom left corner of the Fabric L rectangle.

Leaf Unit should measure 1 ½" x 1 ¾" (2 ½" x 3").

Make two.

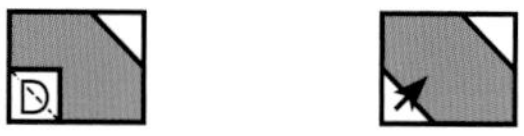

Make two.

Assemble one Leaf Unit, one Fabric M rectangle and one Fabric A rectangle.

Leaf/Stem Unit should measure 1 ½" x 3 ½" (2 ½" x 6 ½").

Make two.

Make two.

With right sides facing, layer a Fabric D square on the top left corner of the Fabric F rectangle.

Stitch on the drawn line and trim ¼" away from the seam.

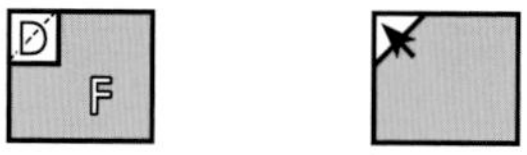

Make one.

Repeat on the top right corner of the Fabric F rectangle.

Partial Middle Left Pear Unit should measure 2 ¼" x 2 ½" (4" x 4 ½").

Make one.

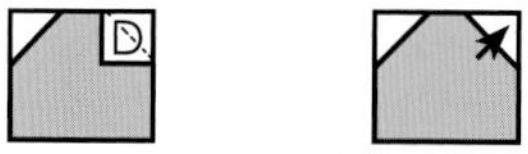

Make one.

Assemble two Fabric C rectangles and the Partial Middle Left Pear Unit.

Middle Left Pear Unit should measure 2 ¼" x 3 ½" (4" x 6 ½").

Make one.

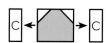

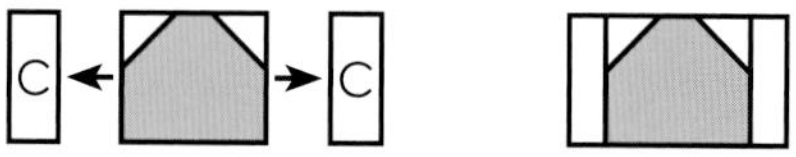

Make one.

Draw a diagonal line on the wrong side of the Fabric B squares.

With right sides facing, layer Fabric D squares on the top left and top right corners of the Fabric E rectangle.

Stitch on the drawn lines and trim ¼" away from the seam.

Make one.

Repeat on the bottom left and bottom right corners of the Fabric E rectangle with the Fabric B squares.

Bottom Left Pear Unit should measure 3 ½" x 3 ¾" (6 ½" x 7").

Make one.

Make one.

Assemble one Leaf/Stem Unit, the Middle Left Pear Unit and the Bottom Left Pear Unit.

Left Pear Unit should measure 3 ½" x 6 ½" (6 ½" x 12 ½").

Make one.

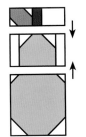 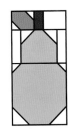

Make one.

With right sides facing, layer a Fabric B square on one end of the Fabric H rectangle.

Stitch on the drawn line and trim ¼" away from the seam.

Make one.

Repeat on the opposite end of the Fabric H rectangle.

Top Right Pear Unit should measure 1 ½" x 3 ½" (2 ½" x 6 ½").

Make one.

Make one.

With right sides facing, layer a Fabric D square on the bottom end of a Fabric I rectangle.

Stitch on the drawn line and trim ¼" away from the seam.

Left Middle Right Pear Unit should measure 1" x 2 ¾" (1 ½" x 5").

Make one.

Make one.

With right sides facing, layer a Fabric D square on the bottom end of a Fabric I rectangle.

Stitch on the drawn line and trim ¼" away from the seam.

Right Middle Right Pear Unit should measure 1" x 2 ¾" (1 ½" x 5").

Make one.

Make one.

Draw a diagonal line on the wrong side of the Fabric J squares.

With right sides facing, layer a Fabric J square on one corner of the Fabric K rectangle.

Stitch on the drawn line and trim ¼" away from the seam.

Make one.

Repeat on the remaining corners of the Fabric K rectangle.

Center Middle Right Pear Unit should measure 2 ½" x 2 ¾" (4 ½" x 5").

Make one.

Make one.

Fresh Pears Block

Assemble the Left Middle Right Pear Unit, the Center Middle Right Pear Unit and the Right Middle Right Pear Unit.

Middle Right Pear Unit should measure 2 ¾" x 3 ½" (5" x 6 ½").

Make one.

Make one.

With right sides facing, layer a Fabric D square on the bottom left corner of the Fabric G rectangle.

Stitch on the drawn line and trim ¼" away from the seam.

Make one.

Repeat on the bottom right corner of the Fabric G rectangle.

Partial Bottom Right Pear Unit should measure 2 ¼" x 2 ½" (4" x 4 ½").

Make one.

Make one.

Assemble two Fabric C rectangles and the Partial Bottom Right Pear Unit.

Bottom Right Pear Unit should measure 2 ¼" x 3 ½" (4" x 6 ½").

Make one.

Make one.

Assemble the Top Right Pear Unit, the Middle Right Pear Unit, the Bottom Right Pear Unit and one Leaf/Stem Unit.

Right Pear Unit should measure 3 ½" x 6 ½" (6 ½" x 12 ½").

Make one.

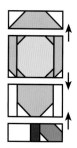 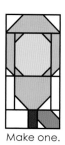

Make one.

Assemble the Fresh Pears Block.

Fresh Pears Block should measure 6 ½" x 6 ½" (12 ½" x 12 ½").

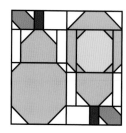 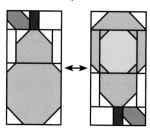
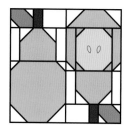

Embroider using three strands of embroidery floss and a backstitch.

6" Right Pear Seeds

12" Right Pear Seeds

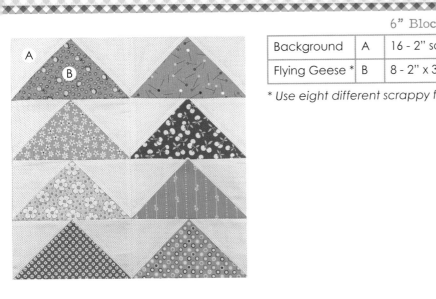

		6" Block	12" Block
Background	A	16 - 2" squares	16 - 3 ½" squares
Flying Geese *	B	8 - 2" x 3 ½" rectangles	8 - 3 ½" x 6 ½" rectangles

* Use eight different scrappy fabrics.

Piecing Instructions:

Draw a diagonal line on the wrong side of the Fabric A squares.

With right sides facing, layer a Fabric A square on one end of a Fabric B rectangle.

Stitch on the drawn line and trim ¼" away from the seam.

Make eight.

Repeat on the opposite end of the Fabric B rectangle.

Flying Geese Unit should measure 2" x 3 ½" (3 ½" x 6 ½").

Make eight.

Make eight.

Assemble four Flying Geese Units.

Flying Geese Row should measure 3 ½" x 6 ½" (6 ½" x 12 ½").

Make two.

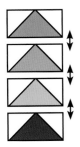 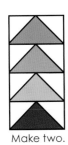

Make two.

Assemble the Furrows Block.

Furrows Block should measure 6 ½" x 6 ½" (12 ½" x 12 ½").

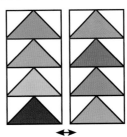 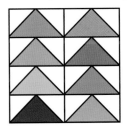

Gingham Block

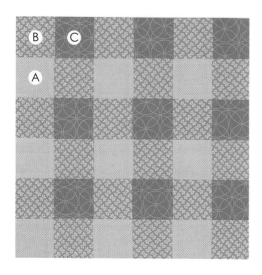

		6" Block	12" Block
Background	A	9 - 1 ½" squares	9 - 2 ½" squares
Medium	B	18 - 1 ½" squares	18 - 2 ½" squares
Dark	C	9 - 1 ½" squares	9 - 2 ½" squares

Piecing Instructions:

Assemble three Fabric B squares and three Fabric C squares.

Gingham Row One Unit should measure 1 ½" x 6 ½" (2 ½" x 12 ½").

Make three.

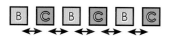 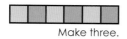

Make three.

Assemble three Fabric A squares and three Fabric B squares.

Gingham Row Two Unit should measure 1 ½" x 6 ½" (2 ½" x 12 ½").

Make three.

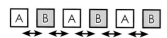 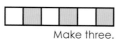

Make three.

Assemble the Gingham Block.

Gingham Block should measure 6 ½" x 6 ½" (12 ½" x 12 ½").

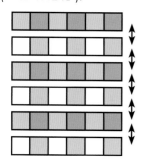 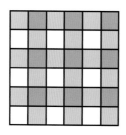

Grandma's Quilt Block

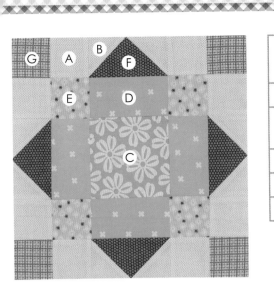

		6" Block	12" Block
Background	A	8 - 1 ½" squares	8 - 2 ½" squares
	B	8 - 1 ½" squares	8 - 2 ½" squares
Center	C	1 - 2 ½" square	1 - 4 ½" square
Rectangles	D	4 - 1 ½" x 2 ½" rectangles	4 - 2 ½" x 4 ½" rectangles
Squares	E	4 - 1 ½" squares	4 - 2 ½" squares
Flying Geese	F	4 - 1 ½" x 2 ½" rectangles	4 - 2 ½" x 4 ½" rectangles
Corners	G	4 - 1 ½" squares	4 - 2 ½" squares

Piecing Instructions:

Draw a diagonal line on the wrong side of the Fabric B squares.

With right sides facing, layer a Fabric B square on one end of a Fabric F rectangle.

Stitch on the drawn line and trim ¼" away from the seam.

Make four.

Repeat on the opposite end of the Fabric F rectangle.

Flying Geese Unit should measure 1 ½" x 2 ½" (2 ½" x 4 ½").

Make four.

Make four.

Assemble two Fabric A squares and one Flying Geese Unit.

Outer Grandma's Quilt Unit should measure 1 ½" x 4 ½" (2 ½" x 8 ½").

Make four.

Make four.

Assemble four Fabric E squares, four Fabric D rectangles and the Fabric C square.

Nine Patch Unit should measure 4 ½" x 4 ½" (8 ½" x 8 ½").

Make one.

Make one.

Assemble the Grandma's Quilt Block.

Grandma's Quilt Block should measure 6 ½" x 6 ½" (12 ½" x 12 ½").

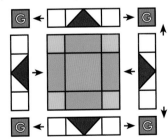 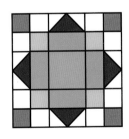

Haystack Block

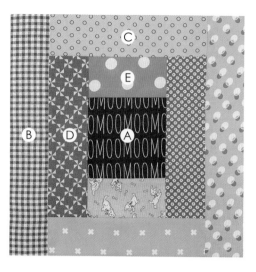

		6" Block	12" Block
Center	A	1 - 2 ½" square	1 - 4 ½" square
Round Four *	B	2 - 1 ½" x 6 ½" rectangles	2 - 2 ½" x 12 ½" rectangles
Round Three *	C	2 - 1 ½" x 4 ½" rectangles	2 - 2 ½" x 8 ½" rectangles
Round Two *	D	2 - 1 ½" x 4 ½" rectangles	2 - 2 ½" x 8 ½" rectangles
Round One *	E	2 - 1 ½" x 2 ½" rectangles	2 - 2 ½" x 4 ½" rectangles

Use two different scrappy fabrics.

Piecing Instructions:

Assemble two Fabric E rectangles and the Fabric A square.

Round One Unit should measure 2 ½" x 4 ½" (4 ½" x 8 ½").

Make one.

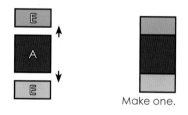

Make one.

Assemble two Fabric D rectangles and the Round One Unit.

Round Two Unit should measure 4 ½" x 4 ½" (8 ½" x 8 ½").

Make one.

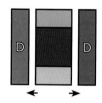

Make one.

Assemble two Fabric C rectangles and the Round Two Unit.

Round Three Unit should measure 4 ½" x 6 ½" (8 ½" x 12 ½").

Make one.

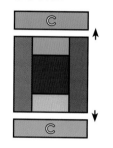
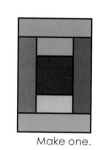

Make one.

Assemble the Haystack Block.

Haystack Block should measure 6 ½" x 6 ½" (12 ½" x 12 ½").

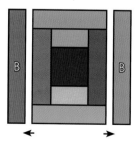
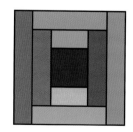

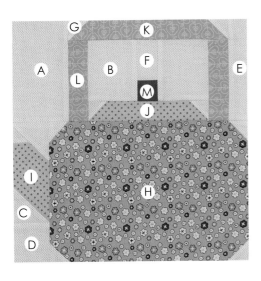

		6" Block	12" Block
Background	A	1 - 2" x 3" rectangle	1 - 3 ½" x 5 ½" rectangle
	B	2 - 1 ¾" x 2" rectangles	2 - 3" x 3 ½" rectangles
	C	2 - 1 ½" squares	2 - 2 ½" squares
	D	1 - 1 ½" square	1 - 2 ½" square
	E	1 - 1" x 3" rectangle	1 - 1 ½" x 5 ½" rectangle
	F	2 - 1" x 1 ½" rectangles	2 - 1 ½" x 2 ½" rectangles
	G	8 - 1" squares	8 - 1 ½" squares
Teapot	H	1 - 4" x 5 ½" rectangle	1 - 7 ½" x 10 ½" rectangle
Spout and Lid	I	1 - 1 ½" x 2 ½" rectangle	1 - 2 ½" x 4 ½" rectangle
	J	1 - 1" x 3 ½" rectangle	1 - 1 ½" x 6 ½" rectangle
Handle	K	1 - 1" x 4 ½" rectangle	1 - 1 ½" x 8 ½" rectangle
	L	2 - 1" x 2 ½" rectangles	2 - 1 ½" x 4 ½" rectangles
Knob	M	1 - 1" square	1 - 1 ½" square

Piecing Instructions:

Draw a diagonal line on the wrong side of the Fabric G squares.

With right sides facing, layer a Fabric G square on one end of the Fabric K rectangle.

Stitch on the drawn line and trim ¼" away from the seam.

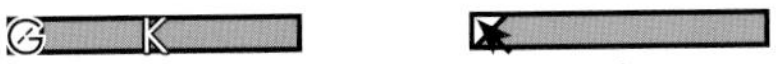

Make one.

Repeat on the opposite end of the Fabric K rectangle.

Top Handle Unit should measure 1" x 4 ½" (1 ½" x 8 ½").

Make one.

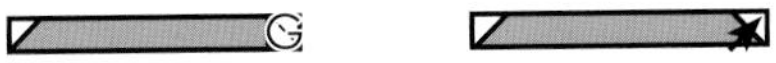

Make one.

With right sides facing, layer a Fabric G square on one end of the Fabric J rectangle.

Stitch on the drawn line and trim ¼" away from the seam.

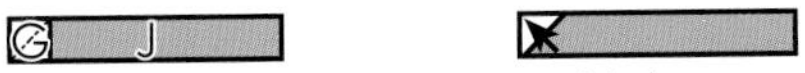

Make one.

Repeat on the opposite end of the Fabric J rectangle.

Lid Unit should measure 1" x 3 ½" (1 ½" x 6 ½").

Make one.

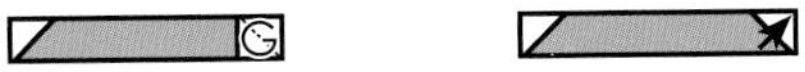

Make one.

Assemble one Fabric F rectangle, the Fabric M square and two Fabric B rectangles.

Knob Unit should measure 2" x 3 ½" (3 ½" x 6 ½").

Make one.

Make one.

Assemble the Knob Unit and the Lid Unit.

Knob/Lid Unit should measure 2 ½" x 3 ½" (4 ½" x 6 ½").

Make one.

Make one.

Assemble two Fabric L rectangles, the Knob/Lid Unit and the Top Handle Unit.

Handle Unit should measure 3" x 4 ½" (5 ½" x 8 ½").

Make one.

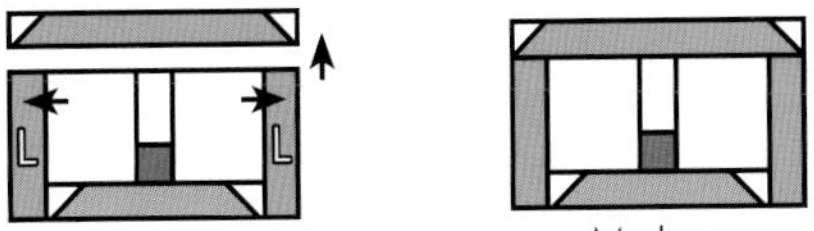

Make one.

Kettle's On! Block

Assemble the Fabric A rectangle, the Handle Unit and the Fabric E rectangle.

Top Kettle's On! Unit should measure 3" x 6 ½" (5 ½" x 12 ½").

Make one.

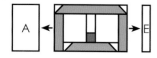 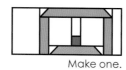

Make one.

Assemble one Fabric F rectangle and the Fabric I rectangle.

Partial Spout Unit should measure 1 ½" x 3" (2 ½" x 5 ½").

Make one.

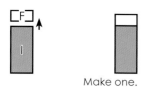

Make one.

Draw a diagonal line on the wrong side of the Fabric C squares.

With right sides facing, layer a Fabric C square on the top end of the Partial Spout Unit.

Pay close attention to unit placement.

Stitch on the drawn line and trim ¼" away from the seam.

Make one.

Repeat on the bottom end of the Partial Spout Unit.

Spout Unit should measure 1 ½" x 3" (2 ½" x 5 ½").

Make one.

Make one.

With right sides facing, layer a Fabric G square on one corner of the Fabric H rectangle.

Stitch on the drawn line and trim ¼" away from the seam.

Make one.

Repeat on the remaining corners of the Fabric H rectangle.

Teapot Unit should measure 4" x 5 ½" (7 ½" x 10 ½").

Make one.

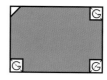 

Make one.

Assemble the Spout Unit, the Fabric D square and the Teapot Unit.

Bottom Kettle's On! Unit should measure 4" x 6 ½" (7 ½" x 12 ½").

Make one.

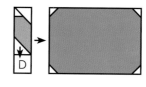 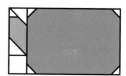

Make one.

Assemble the Kettle's On! Block.

Kettle's On! Block should measure 6 ½" x 6 ½" (12 ½" x 12 ½").

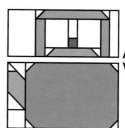 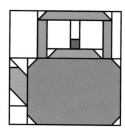

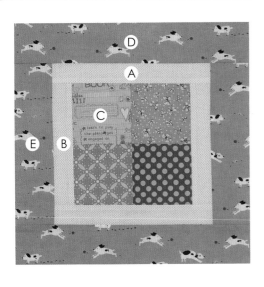

		6" Block	12" Block
Background	A	2 - 1" x 4 ½" rectangles	2 - 1 ½" x 8 ½" rectangles
	B	2 - 1" x 3 ½" rectangles	2 - 1 ½" x 6 ½" rectangles
Window Pane *	C	4 - 2" squares	4 - 3 ½" squares
Window Frame	D	2 - 1 ½" x 6 ½" rectangles	2 - 2 ½" x 12 ½" rectangles
	E	2 - 1 ½" x 4 ½" rectangles	2 - 2 ½" x 8 ½" rectangles

* Use four different scrappy fabrics.

Piecing Instructions:

Assemble four Fabric C squares.

Window Pane Unit should measure 3 ½" x 3 ½" (6 ½" x 6 ½").

Make one.

Make one.

Assemble two Fabric B rectangles, the Window Pane Unit and two Fabric A rectangles.

Center Unit should measure 4 ½" x 4 ½" (8 ½" x 8 ½").

Make one.

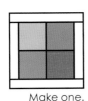

Make one.

Assemble the Kitchen Window Block.

Kitchen Window Block should measure 6 ½" x 6 ½" (12 ½" x 12 ½").

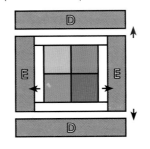

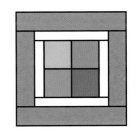

Mama Hen Block

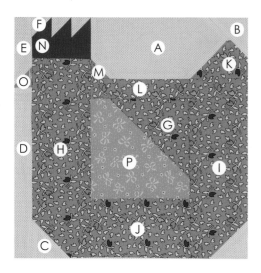

		6" Block	12" Block
Background	A	1 - 2" x 4 ½" rectangle	1 - 3 ½" x 8 ½" rectangle
	B	1 - 1 ½" square	1 - 2 ½" square
	C	2 - 1 ½" squares	2 - 2 ½" squares
	D	1 - 1" x 4 ¾" rectangle	1 - 1 ½" x 9" rectangle
	E	1 - 1" x 2 ¼" rectangle	1 - 1 ½" x 4" rectangle
	F	3 - 1" squares	3 - 1 ½" squares
Hen Body	G	1 - 2 ½" square	1 - 4 ½" square
	H	1 - 2" x 5 ½" rectangle	1 - 3 ½" x 10 ½" rectangle
	I	1 - 2" x 4 ½" rectangle	1 - 3 ½" x 8 ½" rectangle
	J	1 - 2" x 3" rectangle	1 - 3 ½" x 5 ½" rectangle
	K	1 - 2" square	1 - 3 ½" square
	L	1 - 1" x 4 ½" rectangle	1 - 1 ½" x 8 ½" rectangle
	M	1 - 1" square	1 - 1 ½" square
Comb	N	3 - 1" x 1 ½" rectangles	3 - 1 ½" x 2 ½" rectangles
Beak	O	1 - 1" square	1 - 1 ½" square
Wing	P	1 - 3" square	1 - 5 ½" square

Piecing Instructions:

Draw a diagonal line on the wrong side of the Fabric O square.

With right sides facing, layer the Fabric O square on the bottom end of the Fabric E rectangle.

Stitch on the drawn line and trim ¼" away from the seam.

Beak Unit should measure 1" x 2 ¼" (1 ½" x 4").

Make one.

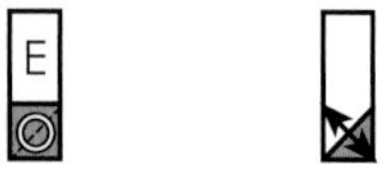

Make one.

Assemble the Beak Unit and the Fabric D rectangle. Left Hen Unit should measure 1" x 6 ½" (1 ½" x 12 ½").

Make one.

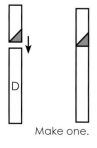

Make one.

Draw a diagonal line on the wrong side of the Fabric F squares.

With right sides facing, layer a Fabric F square on the top end of a Fabric N rectangle.

Stitch on the drawn line and trim ¼" away from the seam.

Partial Comb Unit should measure 1" x 1 ½" (1 ½" x 2 ½").

Make three.

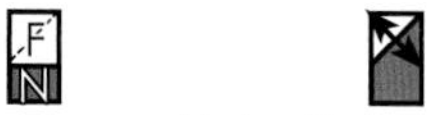

Make three.

Assemble three Partial Comb Units.

Comb Unit should measure 1 ½" x 2" (2 ½" x 3 ½").

Make one.

Make one.

Draw a diagonal line on the wrong side of the Fabric C squares.

With right sides facing, layer a Fabric C square on the bottom left corner of the Fabric H rectangle.

Stitch on the drawn line and trim ¼" away from the seam.

Partial Middle Hen Unit should measure 2" x 5 ½" (3 ½" x 10 ½").

Make one.

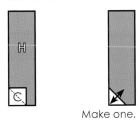

Make one.

Assemble the Comb Unit and the Partial Middle Hen Unit.

Middle Hen Unit should measure 2" x 6 ½" (3 ½" x 12 ½").

Make one.

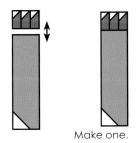

Make one.

Draw a diagonal line on the wrong side of the Fabric M square and the Fabric K square.

With right sides facing, layer the Fabric M square on the bottom left corner of the Fabric A rectangle.

Stitch on the drawn line and trim ¼" away from the seam.

Make one.

Repeat on the right end of the Fabric A rectangle with the Fabric K square.

Partial Feather Unit should measure 2" x 4 ½" (3 ½" x 8 ½").

Make one.

Make one.

Draw a diagonal line on the wrong side of the Fabric B square.

With right sides facing, layer the Fabric B square on the top right corner of the Partial Feather Unit.

Stitch on the drawn line and trim ¼" away from the seam.

Feather Unit should measure 2" x 4 ½" (3 ½" x 8 ½").

Make one.

Make one.

Draw a diagonal line on the wrong side of the Fabric G square.

With right sides facing, layer the Fabric G square on the top right corner of the Fabric P square.

Stitch on the drawn line and trim ¼" away from the seam.

Wing Unit should measure 3" x 3" (5 ½" x 5 ½").

Make one.

Make one.

With right sides facing, layer a Fabric C square on the bottom right corner of the Fabric I rectangle.

Stitch on the drawn line and trim ¼" away from the seam.

Partial Right Hen Unit should measure 2" x 4 ½" (3 ½" x 8 ½").

Make one.

Make one.

Mama Hen Block

Assemble the Wing Unit, the Fabric J rectangle and the Partial Right Hen Unit.

Bottom Right Hen Unit should measure 4 ½" x 4 ½" (8 ½" x 8 ½").

Make one.

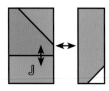

Make one.

Assemble the Feather Unit, the Fabric L rectangle and the Bottom Right Hen Unit.

Right Hen Unit should measure 4 ½" x 6 ½" (8 ½" x 12 ½").

Make one.

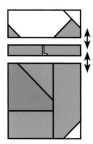 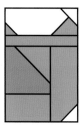

Make one.

Assemble the Mama Hen Block.

Mama Hen Block should measure 6 ½" x 6 ½" (12 ½" x 12 ½").

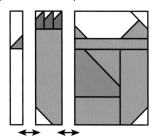 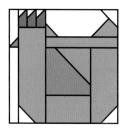

Embroider using three strands of embroidery floss and a backstitch.

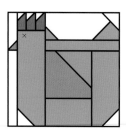

6" Mama Hen Eye

12" Mama Hen Eye

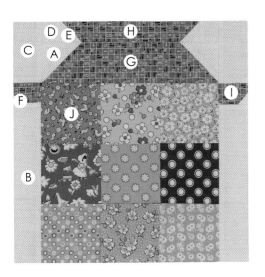

		6" Block	12" Block
Background	A	2 - 1 ½" squares	2 - 2 ½" squares
	B	2 - 1 ¼" x 4 ½" rectangles	2 - 2" x 8 ½" rectangles
	C	2 - 1 ¼" x 2" rectangles	2 - 2" x 3 ½" rectangles
	D	2 - 1" squares	2 - 1 ½" squares
	E	2 - 1" squares	2 - 1 ½" squares
	F	2 - ¾" squares	2 - 1" squares
Milking Top and Handles	G	1 - 1 ½" x 5" rectangle	1 - 2 ½" x 9 ½" rectangle
	H	1 - 1" x 4" rectangle	1 - 1 ½" x 7 ½" rectangle
	I	2 - 1" x 1 ¼" rectangles	2 - 1 ½" x 2" rectangles
Milking Can *	J	9 - 2" squares	9 - 3 ½" squares

Use nine different scrappy fabrics.

Piecing Instructions:

Draw a diagonal line on the wrong side of the Fabric F squares.

With right sides facing, layer a Fabric F square on the bottom left corner of a Fabric I rectangle.

Stitch on the drawn line and trim ¼" away from the seam.

Left Handle Unit should measure 1" x 1 ¼" (1 ½" x 2").

Make one.

Make one.

Assemble one Fabric C rectangle, the Left Handle Unit and one Fabric B rectangle.

Left Milking Day Unit should measure 1 ¼" x 6 ½" (2" x 12 ½").

Make one.

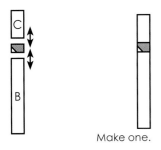

Make one.

With right sides facing, layer a Fabric F square on the bottom right corner of a Fabric I rectangle.

Stitch on the drawn line and trim ¼" away from the seam.

Right Handle Unit should measure 1" x 1 ¼" (1 ½" x 2").

Make one.

Make one.

Assemble one Fabric C rectangle, the Right Handle Unit and one Fabric B rectangle.

Right Milking Day Unit should measure 1 ¼" x 6 ½" (2" x 12 ½").

Make one.

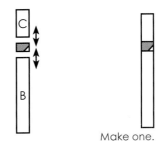

Make one.

Milking Day Block

Draw a diagonal line on the wrong side of the Fabric E squares.

With right sides facing, layer a Fabric E square on one end of the Fabric H rectangle.

Stitch on the drawn line and trim ¼" away from the seam.

Make one.

Repeat on the opposite end of the Fabric H rectangle.

Partial Top Milking Day Unit should measure 1" x 4" (1 ½" x 7 ½").

Make one.

Make one.

Assemble two Fabric D squares and the Partial Top Milking Day Unit.

Top Milking Day Unit should measure 1" x 5" (1 ½" x 9 ½").

Make one.

Make one.

Draw a diagonal line on the wrong side of the Fabric A squares.

With right sides facing, layer a Fabric A square on one end of the Fabric G rectangle.

Stitch on the drawn line and trim ¼" away from the seam.

Make one.

Repeat on the opposite end of the Fabric G rectangle.

Middle Milking Day Unit should measure 1 ½" x 5" (2 ½" x 9 ½").

Make one.

Make one.

Assemble nine Fabric J squares.

Milking Can Unit should measure 5" x 5" (9 ½" x 9 ½").

Make one.

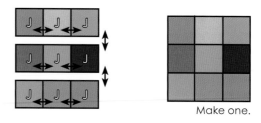

Make one.

Assemble the Top Milking Day Unit, the Middle Milking Day Unit and the Milking Can Unit.

Center Milking Day Unit should measure 5" x 6 ½" (9 ½" x 12 ½").

Make one.

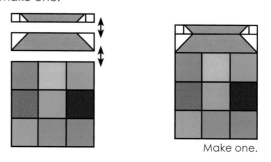

Make one.

Assemble the Milking Day Block.

Milking Day Block should measure 6 ½" x 6 ½" (12 ½" x 12 ½").

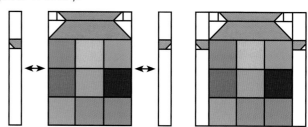

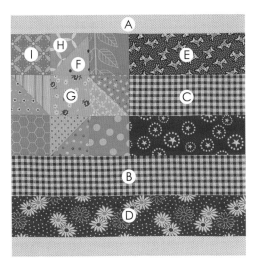

		6" Block	12" Block
Background	A	2 - 1" x 6 ½" rectangles	2 - 1 ½" x 12 ½" rectangles
Gingham Stripes	B	1 - 1 ½" x 6 ½" rectangle	1 - 2 ½" x 12 ½" rectangle
	C	1 - 1 ½" x 3 ½" rectangle	1 - 2 ½" x 6 ½" rectangle
Red Stripes *	D	1 - 1 ½" x 6 ½" rectangle	1 - 2 ½" x 12 ½" rectangle
	E	2 - 1 ½" x 3 ½" rectangles	2 - 2 ½" x 6 ½" rectangles
Star **	F	4 - 1 ½" squares	4 - 2 ½" squares
	G	1 - 1 ½" square	1 - 2 ½" square
Star Background ***	H	4 - 1 ½" squares	4 - 2 ½" squares
	I	4 - 1 ½" squares	4 - 2 ½" squares

* Use three different scrappy fabrics.

** Use five different scrappy fabrics.

*** Use eight different scrappy fabrics.

Piecing Instructions:

Draw a diagonal line on the wrong side of the Fabric F squares.

With right sides facing, layer a Fabric F square with a Fabric H square.

Stitch on the drawn line and trim ¼" away from the seam.

Half Square Triangle Unit should measure 1 ½" x 1 ½" (2 ½" x 2 ½").

Make four.

Make four.

Assemble four Fabric I squares, four Half Square Triangle Units and the Fabric G square.

Star Unit should measure 3 ½" x 3 ½" (6 ½" x 6 ½").

Make one.

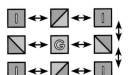

Make one.

Assemble two Fabric E rectangles and the Fabric C rectangle.

Short Stripe Unit should measure 3 ½" x 3 ½" (6 ½" x 6 ½").

Make one.

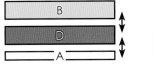

Make one.

Assemble the Fabric B rectangle, the Fabric D rectangle and one Fabric A rectangle.

Long Stripe Unit should measure 3" x 6 ½" (5 ½" x 12 ½").

Make one.

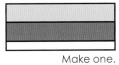

Make one.

Assemble the Old Glory Block.

Old Glory Block should measure 6 ½" x 6 ½" (12 ½" x 12 ½").

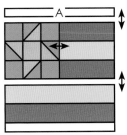

Old Red Barn Block

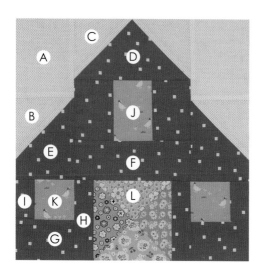

		6" Block	12" Block
Background	A	2 - 2" x 2 ½" rectangles	2 - 3 ½" x 4 ½" rectangles
	B	2 - 2" squares	2 - 3 ½" squares
	C	2 - 2" squares	2 - 3 ½" squares
Barn	D	1 - 2" x 3 ½" rectangle	1 - 3 ½" x 6 ½" rectangle
	E	2 - 2" x 2 ½" rectangles	2 - 3 ½" x 4 ½" rectangles
	F	1 - 1 ½" x 3 ½" rectangle	1 - 2 ½" x 6 ½" rectangle
	G	4 - 1 ½" x 2" rectangles	4 - 2 ½" x 3 ½" rectangles
	H	2 - 1" x 2 ½" rectangles	2 - 1 ½" x 4 ½" rectangles
	I	2 - 1" x 1 ½" rectangles	2 - 1 ½" x 2 ½" rectangles
Barn Windows	J	1 - 1 ½" x 2" rectangle	1 - 2 ½" x 3 ½" rectangle
	K	2 - 1 ½" squares	2 - 2 ½" squares
Door *	L	4 - 3 ½" squares	4 - 5 ½" squares

* Use four different scrappy fabrics.

Piecing Instructions:

Draw a diagonal line on the wrong side of the Fabric B squares.

With right sides facing, layer a Fabric B square on the top end of a Fabric E rectangle.

Stitch on the drawn line and trim ¼" away from the seam.

Left Roof Unit should measure 2" x 2 ½" (3 ½" x 4 ½").

Make one.

Make one.

With right sides facing, layer a Fabric B square on the top end of a Fabric E rectangle.

Stitch on the drawn line and trim ¼" away from the seam.

Right Roof Unit should measure 2" x 2 ½" (3 ½" x 4 ½").

Make one.

Make one.

Assemble one Fabric I rectangle and one Fabric K square.

Small Window Unit should measure 1 ½" x 2" (2 ½" x 3 ½").

Make two.

Make two.

Assemble one Fabric A rectangle, the Left/Right Roof Unit, one Small Window Unit and one Fabric G rectangle.

Pay close attention to unit placement.

Barn Unit should measure 2" x 6 ½" (3 ½" x 12 ½).

Make two total.

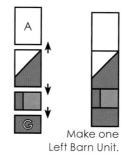

Make one
Left Barn Unit.

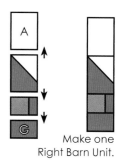

Make one
Right Barn Unit.

Draw a diagonal line on the wrong side of the Fabric C squares.

With right sides facing, layer a Fabric C square on one end of the Fabric D rectangle.

Stitch on the drawn line and trim ¼" away from the seam.

Make one.

Repeat on the opposite end of the Fabric D rectangle.

Flying Geese Unit should measure 2" x 3 ½" (3 ½" x 6 ½").

Make one.

Make one.

Assemble two Fabric G rectangles and the Fabric J rectangle.

Top Window Unit should measure 2" x 3 ½" (3 ½" x 6 ½").

Make one.

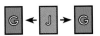

Make one.

Draw a diagonal line on the wrong side of two Fabric L squares.

With right sides facing, layer two Fabric L squares.

Stitch ¼" from each side of the drawn line.

Cut apart on the marked line.

Half Square Triangle Unit should measure 3 ⅛" x 3 ⅛" (5 ⅛" x 5 ⅛").

Make four.

You will use one from each pair.

Make four.

With right sides facing, layer two Half Square Triangle Units.

Make sure they are turned so that the seams are in the same direction.

Make one.

Make one.

Draw diagonal lines ¼" away from the center on the wrong side of one of the Half Square Triangle Units in the opposite direction of the sewn seams. Using a ½" x 6" ruler is helpful.

Stitch on the two drawn lines and cut apart between the stitched lines.

Partial Hourglass Unit should measure 2 ¾" x 2 ¾" (4 ¾" x 4 ¾").

Make two.

You will use one Partial Hourglass Unit.

Make two.

Use a 2 ½" (4 ½") square ruler and trim the Partial Hourglass Unit down to 2 ½" x 2 ½" (4 ½" x 4 ½").

Make one Hourglass Unit.

Make one.

Assemble two Fabric H rectangles and the Hourglass Unit.

Barn Door Unit should measure 2 ½" x 3 ½" (4 ½" x 6 ½").

Make one.

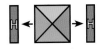

Make one.

Assemble the Old Red Barn Block.

Old Red Barn Block should measure 6 ½" x 6 ½" (12 ½" x 12 ½").

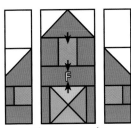 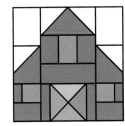

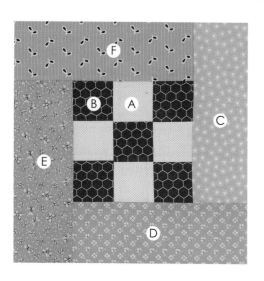

		6" Block	12" Block
Background	A	4 - 1 ½" squares	4 - 2 ½" squares
Nine Patch	B	5 - 1 ½" squares	5 - 2 ½" squares
Right	C	1 - 2" x 5" rectangle	1 - 3 ½" x 9 ½" rectangle
Bottom	D	1 - 2" x 5" rectangle	1 - 3 ½" x 9 ½" rectangle
Left	E	1 - 2" x 5" rectangle	1 - 3 ½" x 9 ½" rectangle
Top	F	1 - 2" x 5" rectangle	1 - 3 ½" x 9 ½" rectangle

Piecing Instructions:

Assemble five Fabric B squares and four Fabric A squares.

Nine Patch Unit should measure 3 ½" x 3 ½" (6 ½" x 6 ½").

Make one.

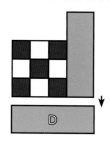

Make one.

Sew the Fabric C rectangle to the Nine Patch Unit.

Start stitching ¼" away from the top. Backstitch.

Make one Out to Pasture Unit One.

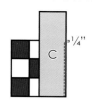

Make one.

Assemble the Out to Pasture Unit One and the Fabric D rectangle.

Make one Out to Pasture Unit Two.

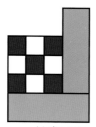

Make one.

Assemble the Fabric E rectangle and the Out to Pasture Unit Two.

Make one Out to Pasture Unit Three.

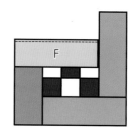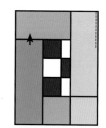

Make one.

Assemble the Out to Pasture Block.

Out to Pasture Block should measure 6 ½" x 6 ½" (12 ½" x 12 ½").

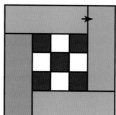

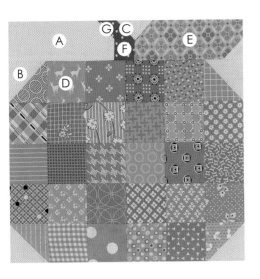

		6" Block	12" Block
Background	A	1 - 1 ½" x 3 ¼" rectangle	1 - 2 ½" x 6" rectangle
	B	4 - 1 ½" squares	4 - 2 ½" squares
	C	3 - 1" squares	3 - 1 ½" squares
Pumpkin *	D	30 - 1 ½" squares	30 - 2 ½" squares
Leaf	E	1 - 1 ½" x 3 ¼" rectangle	1 - 2 ½" x 6" rectangle
Stem	F	1 - 1" x 1 ½" rectangle	1 - 1 ½" x 2 ½" rectangle
	G	1 - 1" square	1 - 1 ½" square

* Use thirty different scrappy fabrics.

Piecing Instructions:

Draw a diagonal line on the wrong side of the Fabric G square.

With right sides facing, layer the Fabric G square on the top right corner of the Fabric A rectangle.

Stitch on the drawn line and trim ¼" away from the seam.

Left Stem Unit should measure 1 ½" x 3 ¼" (2 ½" x 6").

Make one.

Make one.

Draw a diagonal line on the wrong side of the Fabric C squares.

With right sides facing, layer a Fabric C square on the top end of the Fabric F rectangle.

Stitch on the drawn line and trim ¼" away from the seam.

Right Stem Unit should measure 1" x 1 ½" (1 ½" x 2 ½").

Make one.

Make one.

With right sides facing, layer a Fabric C square on the top left corner of the Fabric E rectangle.

Stitch on the drawn line and trim ¼" away from the seam.

Make one.

Repeat on the bottom right corner of the Fabric E rectangle.

Leaf Unit should measure 1 ½" x 3 ¼" (2 ½" x 6").

Make one.

Make one.

Assemble the Left Stem Unit, the Right Stem Unit and the Leaf Unit.

Top Pumpkin Unit should measure 1 ½" x 6 ½" (2 ½" x 12 ½").

Make one.

Make one.

Patchwork Pumpkin Block

Assemble thirty Fabric D squares.

Press rows in alternating directions.

Partial Bottom Pumpkin Unit should measure 5 ½" x 6 ½" (10 ½" x 12 ½").

Make one.

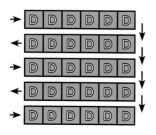
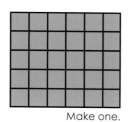

Make one.

Draw a diagonal line on the wrong side of the Fabric B squares.

With right sides facing, layer a Fabric B square on one corner of the Partial Bottom Pumpkin Unit.

Stitch on the drawn line and trim ¼" away from the seam.

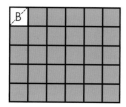
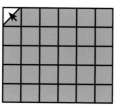

Make one.

Repeat on the remaining corners of the Partial Bottom Pumpkin Unit.

Bottom Pumpkin Unit should measure 5 ½" x 6 ½" (10 ½" x 12 ½").

Make one.

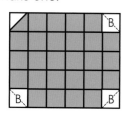
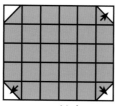

Make one.

Assemble the Patchwork Pumpkin Block.

Patchwork Pumpkin Block should measure 6 ½" x 6 ½" (12 ½" x 12 ½").

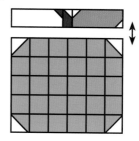
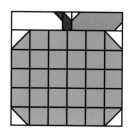

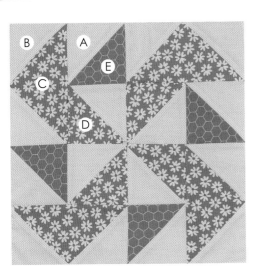

		6" Block	12" Block
Background	A	8 - 2" squares	8 - 3 ½" squares
	B	8 - 2" squares	8 - 3 ½" squares
Carrots	C	4 - 2" x 3 ½" rectangles	4 - 3 ½" x 6 ½" rectangles
	D	4 - 2" squares	4 - 3 ½" squares
Peas	E	4 - 2" squares	4 - 3 ½" squares

Piecing Instructions:

Draw a diagonal line on the wrong side of the Fabric B squares.

With right sides facing, layer a Fabric B square on the top end of a Fabric C rectangle.

Stitch on the drawn line and trim ¼" away from the seam.

Make four.

Repeat on the bottom end of the Fabric C rectangle.

Flying Geese Unit should measure 2" x 3 ½" (3 ½" x 6 ½").
Make four.

Make four.

Draw a diagonal line on the wrong side of the Fabric A squares.

With right sides facing, layer a Fabric A square with a Fabric E square.

Stitch on the drawn line and trim ¼" away from the seam.

Green Half Square Triangle Unit should measure 2" x 2" (3 ½" x 3 ½").

Make four.

Make four.

With right sides facing, layer a Fabric A square with a Fabric D square.

Stitch on the drawn line and trim ¼" away from the seam.

Orange Half Square Triangle Unit should measure 2" x 2" (3 ½" x 3 ½").

Make four.

Make four.

Assemble one Green Half Square Triangle Unit, one Orange Half Square Triangle Unit and one Flying Geese Unit.

Peas and Carrots Unit should measure 3 ½" x 3 ½" (6 ½" x 6 ½").

Make four.

Make four.

Assemble the Peas and Carrots Block.

Peas and Carrots Block should measure 6 ½" x 6 ½" (12 ½" x 12 ½").

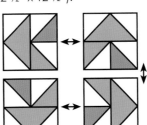 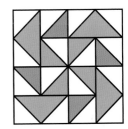

Pie Cherries Block

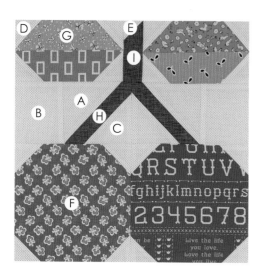

		6" Block	12" Block
Background	A	2 - 2" squares	2 - 3 ½" squares
	B	2 - 1 ¾" x 2" rectangles	2 - 3" x 3 ½" rectangles
	C	2 - 1 ¾" squares	2 - 3" squares
	D	16 - 1 ¼" squares	16 - 2" squares
	E	1 - 1" square	1 - 1 ½" square
Cherries *	F	2 - 3 ½" squares	2 - 6 ½" squares
Leaves **	G	4 - 1 ¼" x 3 ¼" rectangles	4 - 2" x 6" rectangles
Stem	H	2 - 2" x 2 ¼" rectangles	2 - 3 ½" x 4" rectangles
	I	1 - 1" x 2" rectangle	1 - 1 ½" x 3 ½" rectangle

Use two different scrappy fabrics.

**Use four different scrappy fabrics.*

Piecing Instructions:

Draw a diagonal line on the wrong side of the Fabric D squares.

With right sides facing, layer a Fabric D square on one end of a Fabric G rectangle.

Stitch on the drawn line and trim ¼" away from the seam.

Make four.

Repeat on the opposite end of the Fabric G rectangle.

Half Leaf Unit should measure 1 ¼" x 3 ¼" (2" x 6").

Make four.

Make four.

Assemble two Half Leaf Units.

Leaf Unit should measure 2" x 3 ¼" (3 ½" x 6").

Make two.

Make two.

Draw a diagonal line on the wrong side of the Fabric E square.

With right sides facing, layer the Fabric E square on the top end of the Fabric I rectangle.

Stitch on the drawn line and trim ¼" away from the seam.

Stem Unit should measure 1" x 2" (1 ½" x 3 ½").

Make one.

Make one.

Assemble two Leaf Units and the Stem Unit.

Top Pie Cherries Unit should measure 2" x 6 ½" (3 ½" x 12 ½").

Make one.

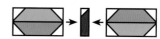 

Make one.

Draw a diagonal line on the wrong side of the Fabric A squares and the Fabric C squares.

With right sides facing, layer a Fabric A square on the left end of a Fabric H rectangle.

Stitch on the drawn line and trim ¼" away from the seam.

Make one.

Repeat on the bottom right corner with a Fabric C square.

Left Stem Unit should measure 2" x 2 ¼" (3 ½" x 4").

Make one.

Make one.

With right sides facing, layer a Fabric A square on the right end of a Fabric H rectangle.

Stitch on the drawn line and trim ¼" away from the seam.

Make one.

Repeat on the bottom left corner with a Fabric C square.

Right Stem Unit should measure 2" x 2 ¼" (3 ½" x 4").

Make one.

Make one.

Assemble two Fabric B rectangles, the Left Stem Unit and the Right Stem Unit.

Middle Pie Cherries Unit should measure 2" x 6 ½" (3 ½" x 12 ½").

Make one.

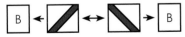 

Make one.

With right sides facing, layer a Fabric D square on one corner of a Fabric F square.

Stitch on the drawn line and trim ¼" away from the seam.

Make two.

Repeat on the remaining corners of the Fabric F square.

Cherry Unit should measure 3 ½" x 3 ½" (6 ½" x 6 ½").

Make two.

Make two.

Assemble two Cherry Units.

Bottom Pie Cherries Unit should measure 3 ½" x 6 ½" (6 ½" x 12 ½").

Make one.

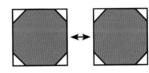 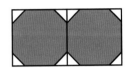

Make one.

Assemble the Pie Cherries Block.

Pie Cherries Block should measure 6 ½" x 6 ½" (12 ½" x 12 ½").

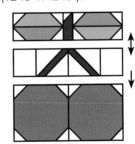 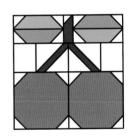

Pinwheels Block

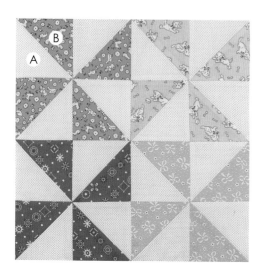

		6" Block	12" Block
Background	A	4 - 4" squares	4 - 7" squares
Pinwheels *	B	4 - 4" squares	4 - 7" squares

* Use four different scrappy fabrics.

Piecing Instructions:

Draw a diagonal line twice on the wrong side of the Fabric A squares.

Make four.

Make four.

With right sides facing, layer a Fabric A square with a Fabric B square.

Stitch on the drawn lines.

Make four Partial Fabric A/B Units.

Make four.

Cut the Partial Fabric A/B Units into quarters.

Fabric A/B Unit should measure 2" x 2" (3 ½" x 3 ½").

Make sixteen.

Make sixteen.

Trim ¼" away from the seam.

Half Square Triangle Unit should measure 2" x 2" (3 ½" x 3 ½").

Make sixteen.

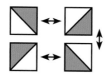

Make sixteen.

Assemble four matching Half Square Triangle Units.

Pinwheel Unit should measure 3 ½" x 3 ½" (6 ½" x 6 ½").

Make four.

Make four.

Assemble the Pinwheels Block.

Pinwheels Block should measure 6 ½" x 6 ½" (12 ½" x 12 ½").

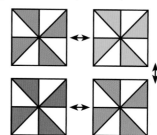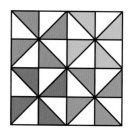

Postage Stamp Block

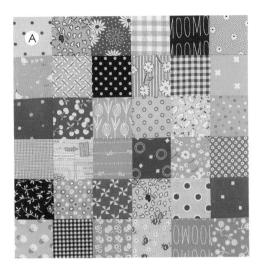

		6" Block	12" Block
Postage Stamps *	A	36 - 1 ½" squares	36 - 2 ½" squares

* Use thirty-six different scrappy fabrics.

Piecing Instructions:

Assemble six Fabric A squares.

Postage Stamp Unit should measure 1 ½" x 6 ½" (2 ½" x 12 ½").

Make six.

Make six.

- -

Assemble the Postage Stamp Block.

Postage Stamp Block should measure 6 ½" x 6 ½" (12 ½" x 12 ½").

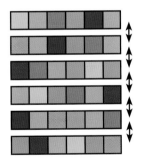   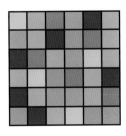

Scrappy Maple Leaf Block

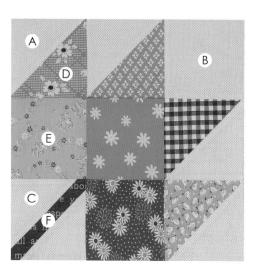

		6" Block	12" Block
Background	A	4 - 2 ½" squares	4 - 4 ½" squares
	B	1 - 2 ½" square	1 - 4 ½" square
	C	2 - 2 ¼" squares	2 - 4" squares
Leaf Tips *	D	4 - 2 ½" squares	4 - 4 ½" squares
Leaf Center **	E	3 - 2 ½" squares	3 - 4 ½" squares
Stem	F	1 - 2 ½" square	1 - 4 ½" square

* Use four different scrappy fabrics.

** Use three different scrappy fabrics.

Piecing Instructions:

Draw a diagonal line on the wrong side of the Fabric A squares.

With right sides facing, layer a Fabric A square with a Fabric D square.

Stitch on the drawn line and trim ¼" away from the seam.

Leaf Tip Unit should measure 2 ½" x 2 ½" (4 ½" x 4 ½").

Make four.

Make four.

Draw a diagonal line on the wrong side of the Fabric C squares.

With right sides facing, layer a Fabric C square on the top left corner of the Fabric F square.

Stitch on the drawn line and trim ¼" away from the seam.

Make one.

Repeat on the bottom right corner of the Fabric F square.

Stem Unit should measure 2 ½" x 2 ½" (4 ½" x 4 ½").

Make one.

Make one.

Assemble the Scrappy Maple Leaf Block.

Scrappy Maple Leaf Block should measure 6 ½" x 6 ½" (12 ½" x 12 ½").

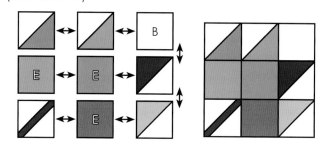

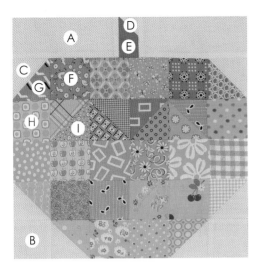

		6" Block	12" Block
Background	A	2 - 1 ½" x 3 ¼" rectangles	2 - 2 ½" x 6" rectangles
	B	2 - 1 ½" squares	2 - 2 ½" squares
	C	6 - 1 ½" squares	6 - 2 ½" squares
	D	1 - 1" square	1 - 1 ½" square
Stem	E	1 - 1" x 1 ½" rectangle	1 - 1 ½" x 2 ½" rectangle
Strawberry Top *	F	4 - 1 ½" squares	4 - 2 ½" squares
	G	6 - 1 ½" squares	6 - 2 ½" squares
Strawberry **	H	14 - 1 ½" squares	14 - 2 ½" squares
	I	8 - 1 ½" squares	8 - 2 ½" squares

Use ten different scrappy fabrics.

** Use twenty-two different scrappy fabrics.

Piecing Instructions:

Draw a diagonal line on the wrong side of the Fabric C squares.

With right sides facing, layer a Fabric C square with a Fabric G square.

Stitch on the drawn line and trim ¼" away from the seam.

Green Half Square Triangle Unit should measure 1 ½" x 1 ½" (2 ½" x 2 ½").

Make two.

Make two.

With right sides facing, layer a Fabric C square with a Fabric I square.

Stitch on the drawn line and trim ¼" away from the seam.

Pink Half Square Triangle Unit should measure 1 ½" x 1 ½" (2 ½" x 2 ½").

Make four.

Make four.

Draw a diagonal line on the wrong side of the remaining Fabric I squares.

With right sides facing, layer a Fabric I square with a Fabric G square.

Stitch on the drawn line and trim ¼" away from the seam.

Green/Pink Half Square Triangle Unit should measure 1 ½" x 1 ½" (2 ½" x 2 ½").

Make four.

Make four.

Draw a diagonal line on the wrong side of the Fabric D square.

With right sides facing, layer the Fabric D square on the top end of the Fabric E rectangle.

Stitch on the drawn line and trim ¼" away from the seam.

Stem Unit should measure 1" x 1 ½" (1 ½" x 2 ½").

Make one.

Make one.

Assemble two Fabric A rectangles and the Stem Unit.
Strawberry Top Unit should measure 1 ½" x 6 ½"
(2 ½" x 12 ½").

Make one.

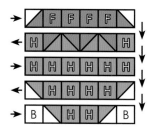 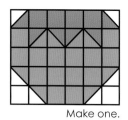

Make one.

Assemble the Strawberry Bottom Unit.

Press rows in alternating directions.

Strawberry Bottom Unit should measure 5 ½" x 6 ½"
(10 ½" x 12 ½").

Make one.

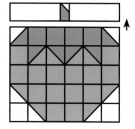 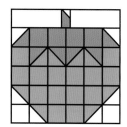

Make one.

Assemble the Scrappy Strawberry Block.

Scrappy Strawberry Block should measure 6 ½" x 6 ½"
(12 ½" x 12 ½").

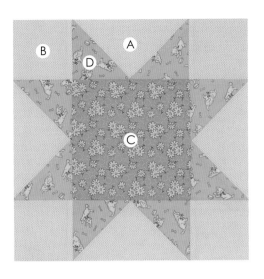

		6" Block	12" Block
Background	A	1 - 4 ¼" square	1 - 7 ¼" square
	B	4 - 2" squares	4 - 3 ½" squares
Star Center	C	1 - 3 ½" square	1 - 6 ½" square
Star Points	D	1 - 4 ¾" square	1 - 7 ¾" square

Piecing Instructions:

Draw diagonal lines ¼" away from the center on the wrong side of the Fabric D square. Using a ½" x 6" ruler is helpful.

Make one.

Make one.

Cut the Fabric D square into quarters.

Fabric D Unit should measure 2 ⅜" x 2 ⅜" (3 ⅞" x 3 ⅞").

Make four.

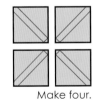

Make four.

Layer two Fabric D Units on opposite ends of the Fabric A square.

Stitch on the two drawn lines and cut apart between the stitched lines.

Make two.

Make two.

Layer one Fabric D Unit on the top right corner of a Fabric D/A Unit.

Stitch on the two drawn lines and cut apart between the stitched lines.

Flying Geese Unit should measure 2" x 3 ½" (3 ½" x 6 ½").

Make four.

Make four.

Assemble the Simple Star Block.

Simple Star Block should measure 6 ½" x 6 ½" (12 ½" x 12 ½").

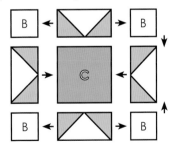 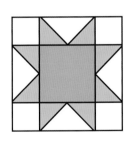

Spring Star Block

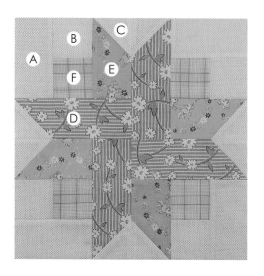

			6" Block	12" Block
Background	A	4 - 1 ½" x 2 ½" rectangles	4 - 2 ½" x 4 ½" rectangles
	B	4 - 1 ½" squares	4 - 2 ½" squares
	C	8 - 1 ½" squares	8 - 2 ½" squares
Green Star Points	D	4 - 1 ½" x 3 ½" rectangles	4 - 2 ½" x 6 ½" rectangles
Pink Star Points	E	4 - 1 ½" x 2 ½" rectangles	4 - 2 ½" x 4 ½" rectangles
Yellow Corners	F	4 - 1 ½" squares	4 - 2 ½" squares

Piecing Instructions:

Draw a diagonal line on the wrong side of the Fabric C squares.

With right sides facing, layer a Fabric C square on the top end of a Fabric E rectangle.

Stitch on the drawn line and trim ¼" away from the seam.

Pink Star Point Unit should measure 1 ½" x 2 ½" (2 ½" x 4 ½").

Make four.

Make four.

With right sides facing, layer a Fabric C square on the left end of a Fabric D rectangle.

Stitch on the drawn line and trim ¼" away from the seam.

Green Star Point Unit should measure 1 ½" x 3 ½" (2 ½" x 6 ½").

Make four.

Make four.

Assemble one Fabric B square and one Fabric F square.
Two Patch Unit should measure 1 ½" x 2 ½" (2 ½" x 4 ½").
Make four.

Make four.

Assemble one Fabric A rectangle, one Two Patch Unit and one Pink Star Point Unit.

Partial Spring Star Unit should measure 2 ½" x 3 ½" (4 ½" x 6 ½").

Make four.

Make four.

Assemble one Partial Spring Star Unit and one Green Star Point Unit.

Spring Star Unit should measure 3 ½" x 3 ½" (6 ½" x 6 ½").

Make four.

Make four.

Assemble the Spring Star Block.

Spring Star Block should measure 6 ½" x 6 ½" (12 ½" x 12 ½").

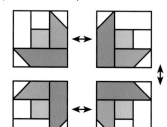

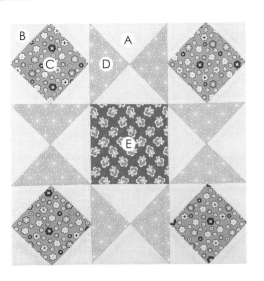

		6" Block	12" Block
Background	A	2 - 3 ½" squares	2 - 5 ½" squares
	B	16 - 1 ½" squares	16 - 2 ½" squares
Diamonds	C	4 - 2 ½" squares	4 - 4 ½" squares
Hourglass	D	2 - 3 ½" squares	2 - 5 ½" squares
Center	E	1 - 2 ½" square	1 - 4 ½" square

Piecing Instructions:

Draw a diagonal line on the wrong side of the Fabric A squares.

With right sides facing, layer a Fabric A square with a Fabric D square.

Stitch ¼" from each side of the drawn line.

Cut apart on the marked line.

Half Square Triangle Unit should measure 3 ⅛" x 3 ⅛" (5 ⅛" x 5 ⅛").

Make four.

Make four.

With right sides facing, layer two Half Square Triangle Units.

Make sure they are turned so that the seams are in the same direction.

Make two.

Make two.

Draw diagonal lines ¼" away from the center on the wrong side of one of the Half Square Triangle Units in the opposite direction of the sewn seams. Using a ½" x 6" ruler is helpful.

Stitch on the two drawn lines and cut apart between the stitched lines.

Partial Hourglass Unit should measure 2 ¾" x 2 ¾" (4 ¾" x 4 ¾").

Make four.

Make four.

Use a 2 ½" (4 ½") square ruler and trim each Partial Hourglass Unit down to 2 ½" x 2 ½" (4 ½" x 4 ½").

Make four Hourglass Units.

Make four.

Draw a diagonal line on the wrong side of the Fabric B squares.

With right sides facing, layer two Fabric B squares on opposite corners of a Fabric C square.

Stitch on the drawn lines and trim ¼" away from the seam.

Make four.

Repeat on the remaining corners of the Fabric C square.

Diamond Unit should measure 2 ½" x 2 ½" (4 ½" x 4 ½").

Make four.

Make four.

Assemble the Summer Star Block.

Summer Star Block should measure 6 ½" x 6 ½" (12 ½" x 12 ½").

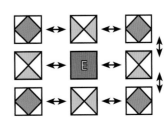 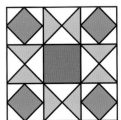

Sunday Morning Block

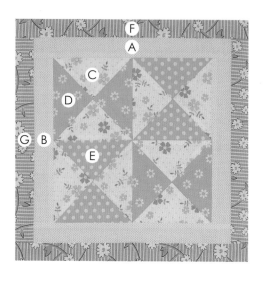

		6" Block	12" Block
Frame	A	2 - 1" x 5 ½" rectangles	2 - 1 ½" x 10 ½" rectangles
	B	2 - 1" x 4 ½" rectangles	2 - 1 ½" x 8 ½" rectangles
Light Hourglass	C	2 - 3 ½" squares	2 - 5 ½" squares
Blue Hourglass	D	1 - 3 ½" square	1 - 5 ½" square
Yellow Hourglass	E	1 - 3 ½" square	1 - 5 ½" square
Border	F	2 - 1" x 6 ½" rectangles	2 - 1 ½" x 12 ½" rectangles
	G	2 - 1" x 5 ½" rectangles	2 - 1 ½" x 10 ½" rectangles

Piecing Instructions:

Draw a diagonal line on the wrong side of the Fabric C squares.

With right sides facing, layer a Fabric C square with a Fabric D square.

Stitch ¼" from each side of the drawn line.

Cut apart on the marked line.

Blue Half Square Triangle Unit should measure 3 ⅛" x 3 ⅛" (5 ⅛" x 5 ⅛").

Make two.

Make two.

With right sides facing, layer two Blue Half Square Triangle Units.

Make sure they are turned so that the seams are in the same direction.

Make one.

Make one.

Draw diagonal lines ¼" away from the center on the wrong side of one of the Blue Half Square Triangle Units in the opposite direction of the sewn seams. Using a ½" x 6" ruler is helpful.

Stitch on the two drawn lines and cut apart between the stitched lines.

Partial Blue Hourglass Unit should measure 2 ¾" x 2 ¾" (4 ¾" x 4 ¾").

Make two.

Make two.

Use a 2 ½" (4 ½") square ruler and trim each Partial Blue Hourglass Unit down to 2 ½" x 2 ½" (4 ½" x 4 ½").

Make two Blue Hourglass Units.

Make two.

With right sides facing, layer a Fabric C square with a Fabric E square.

Stitch ¼" from each side of the drawn line.

Cut apart on the marked line.

Yellow Half Square Triangle Unit should measure 3 ⅛" x 3 ⅛" (5 ⅛" x 5 ⅛").

Make two.

Make two.

With right sides facing, layer two Yellow Half Square Triangle Units.

Make sure they are turned so that the seams are in the same direction.

Make one.

Make one.

Draw diagonal lines ¼" away from the center on the wrong side of one of the Yellow Half Square Triangle Units in the opposite direction of the sewn seams. Using a ½" x 6" ruler is helpful.

Stitch on the two drawn lines and cut apart between the stitched lines.

Partial Yellow Hourglass Unit should measure 2 ¾" x 2 ¾" (4 ¾" x 4 ¾").

Make two.

Make two.

Use a 2 ½" (4 ½") square ruler and trim each Partial Yellow Hourglass Unit down to 2 ½" x 2 ½" (4 ½" x 4 ½").

Make two Yellow Hourglass Units.

Make two.

Assemble two Blue Hourglass Units and two Yellow Hourglass Units.

Pay close attention to unit placement.

Four Patch Hourglass Unit should measure 4 ½" x 4 ½" (8 ½" x 8 ½").

Make one.

Make one.

Assemble two Fabric B rectangles, the Four Patch Hourglass Unit and two Fabric A rectangles.

Sunday Morning Unit should measure 5 ½" x 5 ½" (10 ½" x 10 ½").

Make one.

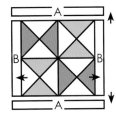

Make one.

Assemble the Sunday Morning Block.

Sunday Morning Block should measure 6 ½" x 6 ½" (12 ½" x 12 ½").

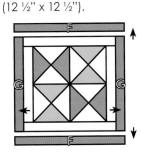 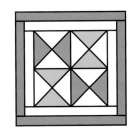

Sunny Sunflower Block

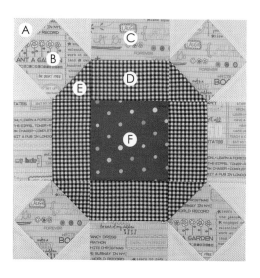

		6" Block	12" Block
Background	A	12 - 1 ½" squares	12 - 2 ½" squares
Sunflower	B	4 - 2 ½" squares	4 - 4 ½" squares
	C	4 - 1 ½" x 2 ½" rectangles	4 - 2 ½" x 4 ½" rectangles
Ring	D	4 - 1 ½" x 2 ½" rectangles	4 - 2 ½" x 4 ½" rectangles
	E	4 - 1 ½" squares	4 - 2 ½" squares
Center	F	1 - 2 ½" square	1 - 4 ½" square

Piecing Instructions:

Draw a diagonal line on the wrong side of the Fabric A squares and the Fabric E squares.

With right sides facing, layer two Fabric A squares on the top right and bottom left corners of a Fabric B square.

Stitch on the drawn lines and trim ¼" away from the seam.

Make four.

Repeat on the top left corner with a Fabric A square and the bottom right corner with a Fabric E square.

Corner Unit should measure 2 ½" x 2 ½" (4 ½" x 4 ½").

Make four.

Make four.

Assemble one Fabric C rectangle and one Fabric D rectangle.

Right Unit should measure 2 ½" x 2 ½" (4 ½" x 4 ½").

Make four.

Make four.

Assemble the Sunny Sunflower Block.

Sunny Sunflower Block should measure 6 ½" x 6 ½" (12 ½" x 12 ½").

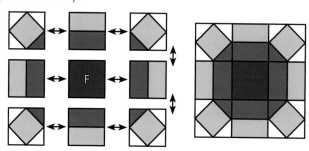

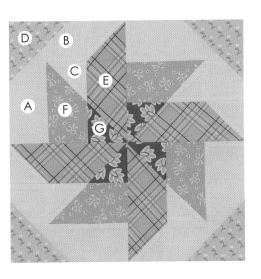

		6" Block	12" Block
Background	A	4 - 1 ½" x 3 ½" rectangles	4 - 2 ½" x 6 ½" rectangles
	B	4 - 1 ½" squares	4 - 2 ½" squares
	C	8 - 1 ½" squares	8 - 2 ½" squares
Corner	D	4 - 2" squares	4 - 3 ½" squares
Green	E	4 - 1 ½" x 3 ½" rectangles	4 - 2 ½" x 6 ½" rectangles
Blue	F	4 - 1 ½" x 2 ½" rectangles	4 - 2 ½" x 4 ½" rectangles
Red	G	4 - 1 ½" squares	4 - 2 ½" squares

Piecing Instructions:

Draw a diagonal line on the wrong side of the Fabric C squares.

With right sides facing, layer a Fabric C square on the top end of a Fabric F rectangle.

Stitch on the drawn line and trim ¼" away from the seam.

Blue Unit should measure 1 ½" x 2 ½" (2 ½" x 4 ½").

Make four.

Make four.

Assemble one Fabric B square and one Blue Unit.

Middle Tumbleweed Unit should measure 1 ½" x 3 ½" (2 ½" x 6 ½").

Make four.

Make four.

Draw a diagonal line on the wrong side of the Fabric G squares.

With right sides facing, layer a Fabric C square on the top end of a Fabric E rectangle.

Stitch on the drawn line and trim ¼" away from the seam.

Make four.

Repeat on the bottom end of the Fabric E rectangle with a Fabric G square.

Right Tumbleweed Unit should measure 1 ½" x 3 ½" (2 ½" x 6 ½").

Make four.

Make four.

Assemble one Fabric A rectangle, one Middle Tumbleweed Unit and one Right Tumbleweed Unit.

Partial Tumbleweed Unit should measure 3 ½" x 3 ½" (6 ½" x 6 ½").

Make four.

Make four.

Draw a diagonal line on the wrong side of the Fabric D squares.

With right sides facing, layer a Fabric D square on the top left corner of a Partial Tumbleweed Unit.

Pay close attention to unit placement.

Stitch on the drawn line and trim ¼" away from the seam.

Tumbleweed Unit should measure 3 ½" x 3 ½" (6 ½" x 6 ½").

Make four.

Make four.

Assemble the Tumbleweed Block.

Tumbleweed Block should measure 6 ½" x 6 ½" (12 ½" x 12 ½").

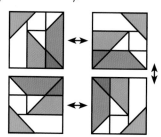 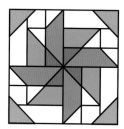

Water Turn Block

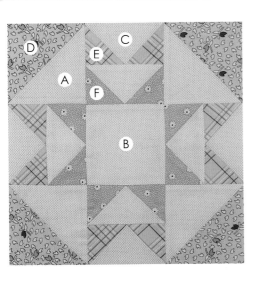

		6" Block	12" Block
Background	A	4 - 2 ½" squares	4 - 4 ½" squares
	B	1 - 2 ½" square	1 - 4 ½" square
	C	8 - 1 ½" x 2 ½" rectangles	8 - 2 ½" x 4 ½" rectangles
Half Square Triangles	D	4 - 2 ½" squares	4 - 4 ½" squares
Green Flying Geese	E	8 - 1 ½" squares	8 - 2 ½" squares
Orange Flying Geese	F	8 - 1 ½" squares	8 - 2 ½" squares

Piecing Instructions:

Draw a diagonal line on the wrong side of the Fabric A squares.

With right sides facing, layer a Fabric A square with a Fabric D square.

Stitch on the drawn line and trim ¼" away from the seam.

Half Square Triangle Unit should measure 2 ½" x 2 ½" (4 ½" x 4 ½").

Make four.

Make four.

Draw a diagonal line on the wrong side of the Fabric E squares.

With right sides facing, layer a Fabric E square on one end of a Fabric C rectangle.

Stitch on the drawn line and trim ¼" away from the seam.

Make four.

Repeat on the opposite end of the Fabric C rectangle.

Green Flying Geese Unit should measure 1 ½" x 2 ½" (2 ½" x 4 ½").

Make four.

Make four.

Draw a diagonal line on the wrong side of the Fabric F squares.

With right sides facing, layer a Fabric F square on one end of a Fabric C rectangle.

Stitch on the drawn line and trim ¼" away from the seam.

Make four.

Repeat on the opposite end of the Fabric C rectangle.

Orange Flying Geese Unit should measure 1 ½" x 2 ½" (2 ½" x 4 ½").

Make four.

Make four.

Assemble the Water Turn Block.

Water Turn Block should measure 6 ½" x 6 ½" (12 ½" x 12 ½").

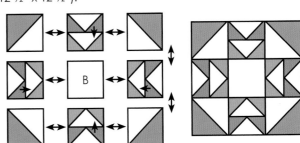

Welcome Block

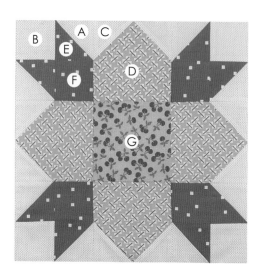

		6" Block	12" Block
Background	A	8 - 1 ½" squares	8 - 2 ½" squares
	B	4 - 1 ½" squares	4 - 2 ½" squares
	C	8 - 1 ½" squares	8 - 2 ½" squares
Points	D	4 - 2 ½" squares	4 - 4 ½" squares
Corners	E	8 - 1 ½" squares	8 - 2 ½" squares
	F	4 - 1 ½" squares	4 - 2 ½" squares
Center	G	1 - 2 ½" square	1 - 4 ½" square

Piecing Instructions:

Draw a diagonal line on the wrong side of the Fabric A squares.

With right sides facing, layer a Fabric A square with a Fabric E square.

Stitch on the drawn line and trim ¼" away from the seam.

Half Square Triangle Unit should measure 1 ½" x 1 ½" (2 ½" x 2 ½").

Make eight.

Make eight.

Assemble one Fabric B square, two Half Square Triangle Units and one Fabric F square.

Corner Unit should measure 2 ½" x 2 ½" (4 ½" x 4 ½").

Make four.

Make four.

Draw a diagonal line on the wrong side of the Fabric C squares.

With right sides facing, layer a Fabric C square on the top left corner of a Fabric D square.

Stitch on the drawn line and trim ¼" away from the seam.

Make four.

Repeat on the top right corner of the Fabric D square.

Point Unit should measure 2 ½" x 2 ½" (4 ½" x 4 ½").

Make four.

Make four.

Assemble the Welcome Block.

Welcome Block should measure 6 ½" x 6 ½" (12 ½" x 12 ½").

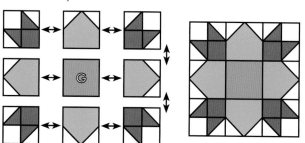

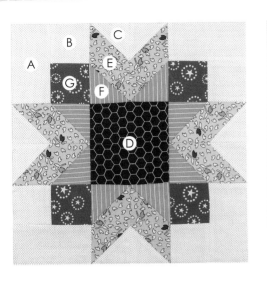

		6" Block	12" Block
Background	A	4 - 1 ½" x 2 ½" rectangles	4 - 2 ½" x 4 ½" rectangles
	B	4 - 1 ½" squares	4 - 2 ½" squares
	C	8 - 1 ½" squares	8 - 2 ½" squares
Center	D	1 - 2 ½" square	1 - 4 ½" square
Blue Star Points	E	8 - 1 ½" x 2 ½" rectangles	8 - 2 ½" x 4 ½" rectangles
Orange Star Points	F	8 - 1 ½" squares	8 - 2 ½" squares
Red Corners	G	4 - 1 ½" squares	4 - 2 ½" squares

Piecing Instructions:

Draw a diagonal line on the wrong side of the Fabric C squares and the Fabric F squares.

With right sides facing, layer a Fabric C square on the top end of a Fabric E rectangle.

Pay close attention to unit placement.

Stitch on the drawn line and trim ¼" away from the seam.

Make four
Left Star Units.

Make four
Right Star Units.

Repeat on the bottom end of the Fabric E rectangle with a Fabric F square.

Star Unit should measure 1 ½" x 2 ½" (2 ½" x 4 ½").

Make eight total.

Make four
Left Star Units.

Make four
Right Star Units.

Assemble one Left Star Unit and one Right Star Unit.

Star Point Unit should measure 2 ½" x 2 ½" (4 ½" x 4 ½").

Make four.

Make four.

Assemble one Fabric B square, one Fabric G square and one Fabric A rectangle.

Corner Unit should measure 2 ½" x 2 ½" (4 ½" x 4 ½").

Make four.

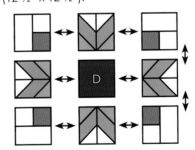

Make four.

Assemble the Winter Star Block.

Winter Star Block should measure 6 ½" x 6 ½" (12 ½" x 12 ½").

Woolly Sheep Block

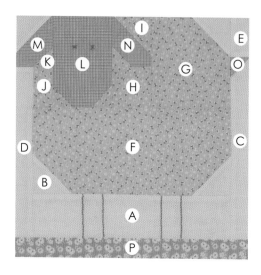

			6" Block	12" Block
Background	A	1 - 1 ½" x 5 ½" rectangle	1 - 2 ½" x 10 ½" rectangle
	B	4 - 1 ½" squares	4 - 2 ½" squares
	C	1 - 1" x 5" rectangle	1 - 1 ½" x 9 ½" rectangle
	D	1 - 1" x 3 ¾" rectangle	1 - 1 ½" x 7" rectangle
	E	2 - 1" x 1 ½" rectangles	2 - 1 ½" x 2 ½" rectangles
Sheep Body	F	1 - 2 ¾" x 5 ½" rectangle	1 - 5" x 10 ½" rectangle
	G	1 - 2 ½" x 2 ¾" rectangle	1 - 4 ½" x 5" rectangle
	H	1 - 1 ½" square	1 - 2 ½" square
	I	1 - 1 ½" square	1 - 2 ½" square
	J	1 - 1" x 1 ½" rectangle	1 - 1 ½" x 2 ½" rectangle
	K	4 - 1" squares	4 - 1 ½" squares
Head and Tail	L	1 - 2" x 2 ¾" rectangle	1 - 3 ½" x 5" rectangle
	M	1 - 1 ½" x 1 ¾" rectangle	1 - 2 ½" x 3" rectangle
	N	1 - 1 ½" x 1 ¾" rectangle	1 - 2 ½" x 3" rectangle
	O	1 - 1" square	1 - 1 ½" square
Grass	P	1 - 1" x 6 ½" rectangle	1 - 1 ½" x 12 ½" rectangle

Piecing Instructions:

Draw a diagonal line on the wrong side of the Fabric B squares and the Fabric K squares.

With right sides facing, layer a Fabric B square on the top end of the Fabric M rectangle.

Stitch on the drawn line and trim ¼" away from the seam.

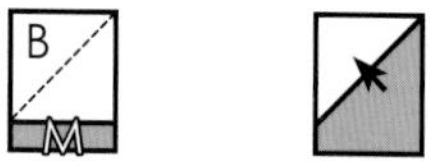

Make one.

Repeat on the bottom right corner of the Fabric M rectangle with a Fabric K square.

Left Ear Unit should measure 1 ½" x 1 ¾" (2 ½" x 3").

Make one.

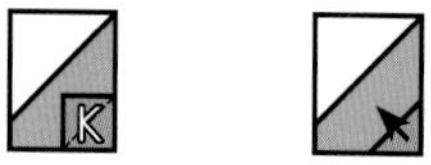

Make one.

Assemble one Fabric E rectangle and the Fabric J rectangle.

Left Sheep Unit should measure 1 ½" x 1 ½" (2 ½" x 2 ½").

Make one.

Make one.

With right sides facing, layer a Fabric K square on the bottom left corner of the Fabric L rectangle.

Stitch on the drawn line and trim ¼" away from the seam.

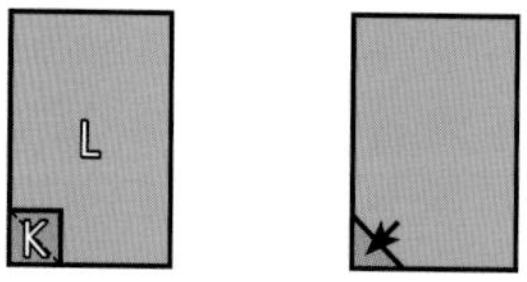

Make one.

Repeat on the bottom right corner of the Fabric L rectangle.

Head Unit should measure 2" x 2 ¾" (3 ½" x 5").

Make one.

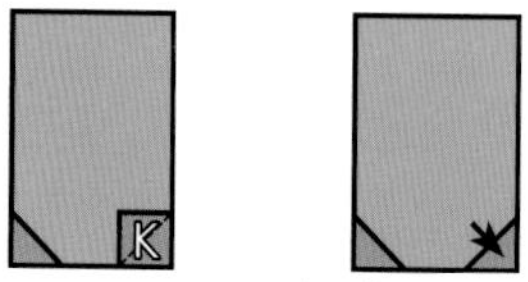

Make one.

Draw a diagonal line on the wrong side of the Fabric I square.

With right sides facing, layer the Fabric I square on the top end of the Fabric N rectangle.

Stitch on the drawn line and trim ¼" away from the seam.

Make one.

Repeat on the bottom left corner of the Fabric N rectangle with a Fabric K square.

Right Ear Unit should measure 1 ½" x 1 ¾" (2 ½" x 3").

Make one.

Make one.

With right sides facing, layer a Fabric B square on the top right corner of the Fabric G rectangle.

Stitch on the drawn line and trim ¼" away from the seam.

Right Sheep Unit should measure 2 ½" x 2 ¾" (4 ½" x 5").

Make one.

Make one.

Assemble the Left Ear Unit, the Left Sheep Unit, the Head Unit, the Right Ear Unit, the Fabric H square and the Right Sheep Unit.

Top Sheep Unit should measure 2 ¾" x 6" (5" x 11 ½").

Make one.

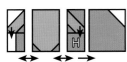 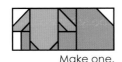

Make one.

Draw a diagonal line on the wrong side of the Fabric O square.

With right sides facing, layer the Fabric O square on the top end of the Fabric C rectangle.

Stitch on the drawn line and trim ¼" away from the seam.

Tail Unit should measure 1" x 5" (1 ½" x 9 ½").

Make one.

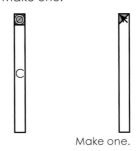

Make one.

Assemble one Fabric E rectangle and the Tail Unit.

Side Unit should measure 1" x 6" (1 ½" x 11 ½").

Make one.

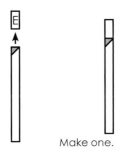

Make one.

With right sides facing, layer a Fabric B square on the bottom left corner of the Fabric F rectangle.

Stitch on the drawn line and trim ¼" away from the seam.

Make one.

Repeat on the bottom right corner of the Fabric F rectangle.

Partial Body Unit should measure 2 ¾" x 5 ½" (5" x 10 ½").

Make one.

Make one.

Woolly Sheep Block

Assemble the Partial Body Unit, the Fabric A rectangle and the Fabric D rectangle.

Middle Body Unit should measure 3 ¾" x 6" (7" x 11 ½").

Make one.

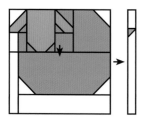

Make one.

Assemble the Top Sheep Unit, the Middle Body Unit and the Side Unit.

Woolly Sheep Unit should measure 6" x 6 ½" (11 ½" x 12 ½").

Make one.

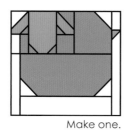

Make one.

Assemble the Woolly Sheep Block.

Woolly Sheep Block should measure 6 ½" x 6 ½" (12 ½" x 12 ½").

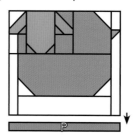 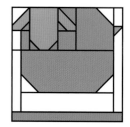

Embroider using three strands of embroidery floss and a backstitch.

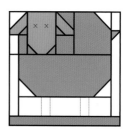

6" Woolly Sheep Eyes

×

6" Woolly Sheep Legs

12" Woolly Sheep Eyes

×

12" Woolly Sheep Legs

Barn & Tractor Blocks and Quilts

Farms are synonymous with barns and silos, and I'm paying homage to them here. Select a medley of your favorite 6" Farm Girl Blocks to set into these little beauties!

Finished size: 14" x 14"

Background	A	2 - 2 ½" x 4 ½" rectangles
	B	2 - 2 ½" squares
	C	1 - 2 ½" square
	D	4 - 1 ½" squares
Barn and Chimneys	E	1 - 2 ½" x 6 ½" rectangle
	F	1 - 2 ½" x 6 ½" rectangle
	G	2 - 2 ½" squares
	H	2 - 1 ½" x 8 ½" rectangles
	I	2 - 1 ½" x 6 ½" rectangles
	J	2 - 1 ½" x 6 ½" rectangles
	K	2 - 1 ½" x 2 ½" rectangles
Roof and Chimneys	L	1 - 4 ½" x 8 ½" rectangle
	M	1 - 2 ½" square
	N	2 - 1 ½" x 2 ½" rectangles
Door	O	1 - 4 ½" x 6 ½" rectangle
Window	P	1 - 2 ½" square

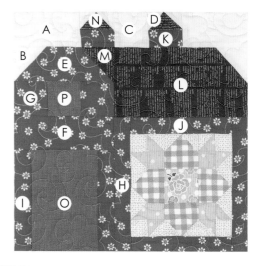

Recipe

Sew your favorite 6" Farm Girl Block from the Farm Girl Blocks section starting on page 8. This block features the Welcome Block from page 70.

Piecing Instructions:

Draw a diagonal line on the wrong side of the Fabric D squares.

With right sides facing, layer a Fabric D square on one end of a Fabric N rectangle.

Stitch on the drawn line and trim ¼" away from the seam.

   Make two.

Repeat on the opposite end of the Fabric N rectangle.

Flying Geese Unit should measure 1 ½" x 2 ½".

Make two.

   Make two.

Assemble one Flying Geese Unit and one Fabric K rectangle.

Chimney Unit should measure 2 ½" x 2 ½".

Make two.

   Make two.

Assemble two Fabric A rectangles, two Chimney Units and the Fabric C square.

Top Quilty Barn Unit should measure 2 ½" x 14 ½".

Make one.

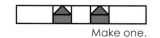   Make one.

Draw a diagonal line on the wrong side of the Fabric B squares and the Fabric M square.

With right sides facing, layer a Fabric B square on the left end of the Fabric E rectangle.

Stitch on the drawn line and trim ¼" away from the seam.

   Make one.

Repeat on the right end of the Fabric E rectangle with the Fabric M square.

Top Window Unit should measure 2 ½" x 6 ½".

Make one.

   Make one.

Assemble two Fabric G squares and the Fabric P square.

Bottom Window Unit should measure 2 ½" x 6 ½".

Make one.

Make one.

Assemble the Top Window Unit and the Bottom Window Unit.

Window Unit should measure 4 ½" x 6 ½".

Make one.

Make one.

With right sides facing, layer a Fabric B square on the top right corner of the Fabric L rectangle.

Stitch on the drawn line and trim ¼" away from the seam.

Right Roof Unit should measure 4 ½" x 8 ½".

Make one.

Make one.

Assemble the Window Unit and the Right Roof Unit.

Middle Quilty Barn Unit should measure 4 ½" x 14 ½".

Make one.

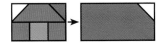 

Make one.

Assemble two Fabric I rectangles and the Fabric O rectangle.

Bottom Door Unit should measure 6 ½" x 6 ½".

Make one.

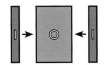

Make one.

Assemble the Fabric F rectangle and the Bottom Door Unit.

Door Unit should measure 6 ½" x 8 ½".

Make one.

Make one.

Assemble two Fabric J rectangles, the 6" Farm Girl Block and two Fabric H rectangles.

Farm Girl Unit should measure 8 ½" x 8 ½".

Make one.

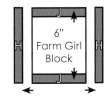

Make one.

Assemble the Door Unit and the Farm Girl Unit.

Bottom Quilty Barn Unit should measure 8 ½" x 14 ½".

Make one.

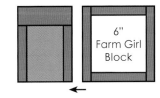 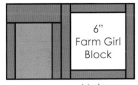

Make one.

Assemble the Quilty Barn Block.

Quilty Barn Block should measure 14 ½" x 14 ½".

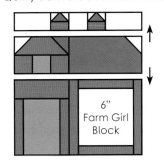 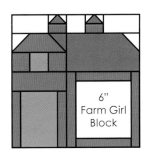

Silo Barn Block

Finished size: 14" x 14"

Background	A	2 - 3 ½" squares	
	B	2 - 2 ½" x 4 ½" rectangles	
	C	4 - 1 ½" squares	
Barn	D	1 - 3 ½" x 6 ½" rectangle	
	E	1 - 3 ½" x 6 ½" rectangle	
	F	2 - 2 ½" x 6 ½" rectangles	
	G	2 - 2 ½" x 4 ½" rectangles	
Chimney and Silo	H	1 - 4 ½" x 12 ½" rectangle	
	I	1 - 1 ½" x 2 ½" rectangle	
Chimney and Silo Roof	J	1 - 2 ½" x 4 ½" rectangle	
	K	1 - 1 ½" x 2 ½" rectangle	
Window	L	1 - 2 ½" x 4 ½" rectangle	

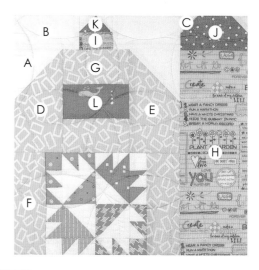

Piecing Instructions:

Draw a diagonal line on the wrong side of the Fabric C squares.

With right sides facing, layer a Fabric C square on one end of the Fabric K rectangle.

Stitch on the drawn line and trim ¼" away from the seam.

Make one.

Repeat on the opposite end of the Fabric K rectangle. Flying Geese Unit should measure 1 ½" x 2 ½".

Make one.

Make one.

Assemble the Flying Geese Unit and the Fabric I rectangle.

Chimney Unit should measure 2 ½" x 2 ½".

Make one.

Make one.

Assemble two Fabric B rectangles and the Chimney Unit.

Top Barn Unit should measure 2 ½" x 10 ½".

Make one.

Make one.

Recipe

Sew your favorite 6" Farm Girl Block from the Farm Girl Blocks section starting on page 8. This block features the Chicken Foot Block from page 18.

Draw a diagonal line on the wrong side of the Fabric A squares.

With right sides facing, layer a Fabric A square on the top end of the Fabric D rectangle.

Stitch on the drawn line and trim ¼" away from the seam.

Left Roof Unit should measure 3 ½" x 6 ½".

Make one.

Make one.

Assemble two Fabric G rectangles and the Fabric L rectangle.

Window Unit should measure 4 ½" x 6 ½".

Make one.

          Make one.

With right sides facing, layer a Fabric A square on the top end of the Fabric E rectangle.

Stitch on the drawn line and trim ¼" away from the seam.

Right Roof Unit should measure 3 ½" x 6 ½".

Make one.

Make one.

Assemble the Left Roof Unit, the Window Unit and the Right Roof Unit.

Middle Barn Unit should measure 6 ½" x 10 ½".

Make one.

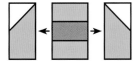

Make one.

Assemble two Fabric F rectangles and the 6" Farm Girl Block.

Bottom Barn Unit should measure 6 ½" x 10 ½".

Make one.

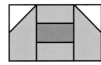

Make one.

Assemble the Top Barn Unit, the Middle Barn Unit and the Bottom Barn Unit.

Barn Unit should measure 10 ½" x 14 ½".

Make one.

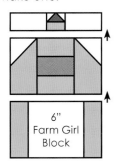

Make one.

With right sides facing, layer a Fabric C square on the top left corner of the Fabric J rectangle.

Stitch on the drawn line and trim ¼" away from the seam.

Make one.

Repeat on the top right corner of the Fabric J rectangle.

Silo Roof Unit should measure 2 ½" x 4 ½".

Make one.

Make one.

Assemble the Silo Roof Unit and the Fabric H rectangle.

Silo Unit should measure 4 ½" x 14 ½".

Make one.

Make one.

Assemble the Silo Barn Block.

Silo Barn Block should measure 14 ½" x 14 ½".

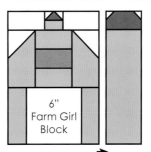

Tractor Block

Finished size: 16" x 20"

Background			
	A	1 - 5 ½" x 7 ½" rectangle	
	B	1 - 4 ½" x 14 ½" rectangle	
	C	1 - 4 ½" x 5 ½" rectangle	
	D	1 - 3 ½" x 5 ½" rectangle	
	E	4 - 2 ½" squares	
	F	1 - 2 ½" square	
	G	1 - 1 ½" x 6 ½" rectangle	
	H	2 - 1 ½" x 2 ½" rectangles	
	I	9 - 1 ½" squares	
Tractor Body	J	1 - 3 ½" x 9 ½" rectangle	
	K	1 - 2 ½" x 10 ½" rectangle	
	L	2 - 2 ½" squares	
	M	1 - 1 ½" x 6 ½" rectangle	
	N	1 - 1 ½" x 4 ½" rectangle	
	O	1 - 1 ½" square	
Tractor Stripe and Wheel Centers	P	1 - 4 ½" square	
	Q	1 - 3 ½" square	
	R	1 - 1 ½" x 10 ½" rectangle	
	S	1 - 1 ½" square	
Tractor Front and Bottom	T	1 - 2 ½" x 6 ½" rectangle	
	U	1 - 1 ½" x 7 ½" rectangle	
Tractor Wheels	V	2 - 2 ½" x 8 ½" rectangles	
	W	2 - 2 ½" x 4 ½" rectangles	
	X	2 - 1 ½" x 5 ½" rectangles	
	Y	2 - 1 ½" x 3 ½" rectangles	
	Z	8 - 1 ½" squares	

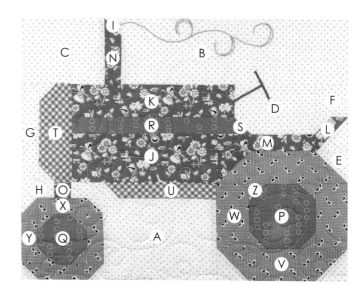

Piecing Instructions:

Draw a diagonal line on the wrong side of the Fabric I squares.

With right sides facing, layer a Fabric I square on the top end of the Fabric N rectangle.

Stitch on the drawn line and trim ¼" away from the seam.

Smokestack Unit should measure 1 ½" x 4 ½".

Make one.

Make one.

Assemble the Fabric C rectangle, the Smokestack Unit and the Fabric B rectangle.

Top Tractor Unit should measure 4 ½" x 20 ½".

Make one.

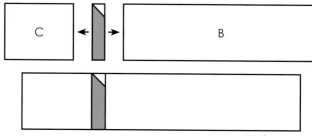

Make one.

With right sides facing, layer a Fabric I square on the top left corner of the Fabric T rectangle.

Stitch on the drawn line and trim ¼" away from the seam.

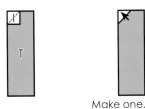

Make one.

Repeat on the bottom left corner of the Fabric T rectangle.

Tractor Front Unit should measure 2 ½" x 6 ½".

Make one.

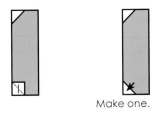

Make one.

Assemble the Fabric G rectangle and the Tractor Front Unit.

Left Middle Tractor Unit should measure 3 ½" x 6 ½".

Make one.

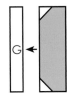

Make one.

Assemble the Fabric K rectangle and the Fabric R rectangle.

Center Middle Tractor Unit should measure 3 ½" x 10 ½".

Make one.

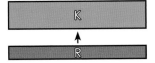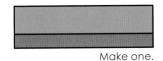

Make one.

Draw a diagonal line on the wrong side of the Fabric S square.

With right sides facing, layer the Fabric S square on the bottom left corner of the Fabric D rectangle.

Stitch on the drawn line and trim ¼" away from the seam.

Right Middle Tractor Unit should measure 3 ½" x 5 ½".

Make one.

Make one.

Assemble the Center Middle Tractor Unit and the Right Middle Tractor Unit.

Top Middle Tractor Unit should measure 3 ½" x 15 ½".

Make one.

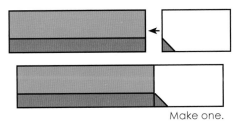

Make one.

Draw a diagonal line on the wrong side of the Fabric E squares.

With right sides facing, layer a Fabric I square on the top left corner of a Fabric L square.

Stitch on the drawn line and trim ¼" away from the seam.

Make one.

Repeat on the bottom right corner of the Fabric L square with a Fabric E square.

Seat Back Unit should measure 2 ½" x 2 ½".

Make one.

Make one.

Assemble the Fabric F square and the Seat Back Unit.
Seat Unit should measure 2 ½" x 4 ½".

Make one.

Make one.

Sew the Top Middle Tractor Unit to the Seat Unit.
Stop stitching 1 ¼" from the end of the unit. Backstitch.
Make one Top Right Middle Tractor Unit.

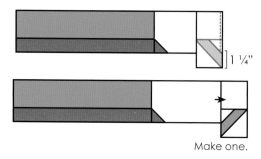

1 ¼"

Make one.

Draw a diagonal line on the wrong side of the remaining Fabric L square.

With right sides facing, layer the Fabric L square on the left end of a Fabric V rectangle.

Stitch on the drawn line and trim ¼" away from the seam.

Make one.

Repeat on the right end of the Fabric V rectangle with a Fabric E square.

Top Large Tire Unit should measure 2 ½" x 8 ½".

Make one.

Make one.

Sew the Fabric M rectangle to the Top Large Tire Unit.
Stop stitching 2 ¼" from the end of the unit. Backstitch.
Make one Bottom Right Tractor Unit.

2 ¼"

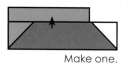

Make one.

Assemble the Fabric J rectangle and the Bottom Right Tractor Unit.

Make one Bottom Right Middle Tractor Unit.

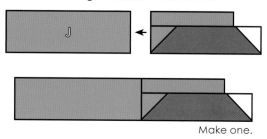

Make one.

Assemble the Top Right Middle Tractor Unit and the Bottom Right Middle Tractor Unit.

Partial Middle Tractor Unit should measure 6 ½" x 17 ½".

Make one.

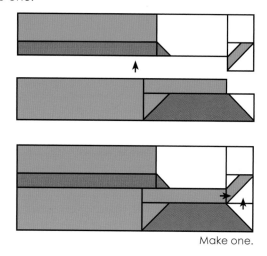

Make one.

Assemble the Left Middle Tractor Unit and the Partial Middle Tractor Unit.

Middle Tractor Unit should measure 6 ½" x 20 ½".

Make one.

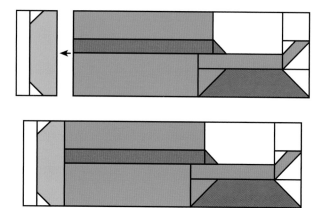

Make one.

Assemble two Fabric H rectangles and the Fabric O square.

Top Small Tire Unit should measure 1 ½" x 5 ½".

Make one.

Make one.

With right sides facing, layer a Fabric I square on one end of a Fabric X rectangle.

Stitch on the drawn line and trim ¼" away from the seam.

Make two.

Repeat on the opposite end of the Fabric X rectangle.

Top and Bottom Small Tire Unit should measure 1 ½" x 5 ½".

Make two.

Make two.

Draw a diagonal line on the wrong side of the Fabric Z squares.

With right sides facing, layer a Fabric Z square on one corner of the Fabric Q square.

Stitch on the drawn line and trim ¼" away from the seam.

Make one.

Repeat on the remaining corners of the Fabric Q square.

Small Hubcap Unit should measure 3 ½" x 3 ½".

Make one.

Make one.

Assemble two Fabric Y rectangles and the Small Hubcap Unit.

Middle Small Tire Unit should measure 3 ½" x 5 ½".

Make one.

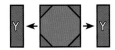
Make one.

Assemble the Top Small Tire Unit, two Top and Bottom Small Tire Units and the Middle Small Tire Unit.

Small Tire Unit should measure 5 ½" x 6 ½".

Make one.

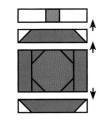
Make one.

With right sides facing, layer a Fabric I square on the left end of the Fabric U rectangle.

Stitch on the drawn line and trim ¼" away from the seam.

Partial Middle Bottom Tractor Unit should measure 1 ½" x 7 ½".

Make one.

Make one.

Assemble the Partial Middle Bottom Tractor Unit and the Fabric A rectangle.

Middle Bottom Tractor Unit should measure 6 ½" x 7 ½".

Make one.

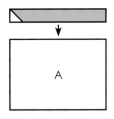 
Make one.

With right sides facing, layer a Fabric E square on one end of a Fabric V rectangle.

Stitch on the drawn line and trim ¼" away from the seam.

Make one.

Repeat on the opposite end of the Fabric V rectangle.

Bottom Large Tire Unit should measure 2 ½" x 8 ½".

Make one.

Make one.

Tractor Block

With right sides facing, layer a Fabric Z square on one corner of the Fabric P square.

Stitch on the drawn line and trim ¼" away from the seam.

Make one.

Repeat on the remaining corners of the Fabric P square.
Large Hubcap Unit should measure 4 ½" x 4 ½".
Make one.

Make one.

Assemble two Fabric W rectangles and the Large Hubcap Unit.
Middle Large Tire Unit should measure 4 ½" x 8 ½".
Make one.

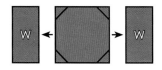 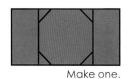

Make one.

Assemble the Middle Large Tire Unit and the Bottom Large Tire Unit.
Large Tire Unit should measure 6 ½" x 8 ½".
Make one.

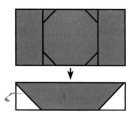 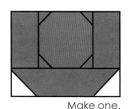

Make one.

Assemble the Small Tire Unit, the Middle Bottom Tractor Unit and the Large Tire Unit.
Bottom Tractor Unit should measure 6 ½" x 20 ½".
Make one.

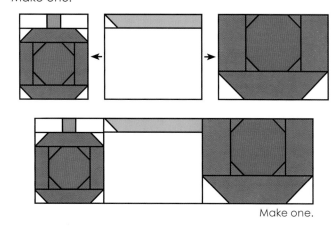

Make one.

Assemble the Tractor Block.
Tractor Block should measure 16 ½" x 20 ½".

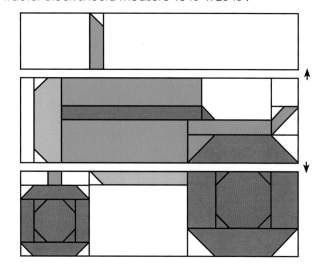

Embroider the tractor steering wheel and smoke using three strands of embroidery floss and a backstitch.

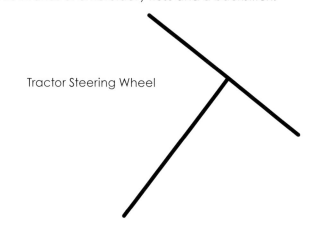

Tractor Steering Wheel

Smoke

Cutting Instructions:

Background (1 ⅛ yards):

- Cut 24	1 ½" x 14 ½" rectangles	Fabric A
- Cut 24	1 ½" x 16 ½" rectangles	Fabric B

Sashing (scraps):

- Cut 24	2 ½" x 16 ½" rectangles	Fabric C
- Cut 24	2 ½" x 20 ½" rectangles	Fabric D

Scrappy Border (scraps):

- Cut 14	2 ½" x 20 ½" rectangles	Fabric E

Border Corners (scraps):

- Cut 4	2 ½" squares	Fabric F

Binding (⅞ yard):

- Cut 9	2 ½" x width of fabric strips	Fabric G

Backing (5 ¼ yards):

- Cut 2	37 ¾" x 94 ½" rectangles	Fabric H

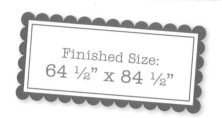

Finished Size:
64 ½" x 84 ½"

Recipe

Sew twelve Quilty Barn Blocks from page 78.

Sashed Quilty Barn Blocks:

Assemble two Fabric A rectangles, one Quilty Barn Block and two Fabric B rectangles.

Framed Quilty Barn Unit should measure 16 ½" x 16 ½".

Make twelve.

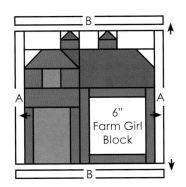
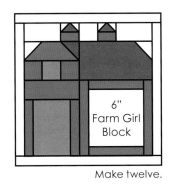

Make twelve.

Assemble two Fabric C rectangles, one Framed Quilty Barn Unit and two Fabric D rectangles.

Pay close attention to fabric placement.

Sashed Quilty Barn One Block should measure 20 ½" x 20 ½".

Make six.

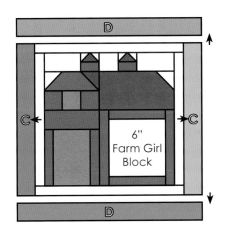
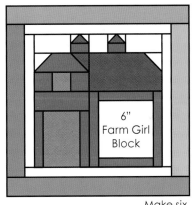

Make six.

Assemble two Fabric C rectangles, one Framed Quilty Barn Unit and two Fabric D rectangles.

Pay close attention to fabric placement.

Sashed Quilty Barn Two Block should measure 20 ½" x 20 ½".

Make six.

Make six.

Quilty Barn Quilt

Quilt Center:

Assemble the Quilt Center.

Use the Fabric E rectangles for scrappy border and the Fabric F squares for border corners. Press rows in alternating directions.

Quilt Center should measure 64 ½" x 84 ½".

Finishing:

Piece the Fabric G strips end to end for binding.

Piece the Fabric H rectangles together with a ½" seam for a vertical backing.
Press open for less bulk.

Quilt and bind as desired.

Silo Barn Quilt

Cutting Instructions:

Background and Inner Border (⅞ yard):

- Cut 24	1 ½" x 14 ½" rectangles	Fabric A
- Cut 36	1 ½" squares	Fabric B
- Cut 2	1 ½" x 37 ½" strips	Fabric C
- Cut 2	1 ½" x 39 ½" strips	Fabric D

Sashing (⅝ yard):

- Cut 12	1 ½" x 14 ½" rectangles	Fabric E

Nine Patch (nine scrappy fabrics):

- Cut 5	1 ½" squares (45 total)	Fabric F

Outer Border (1 ¼ yards):

- Cut 6	6 ½" x width of fabric strips	Fabric G

Binding (⅝ yard):

- Cut 7	2 ½" x width of fabric strips	Fabric H

Backing (3 ½ yards):

- Cut 2	31 ¼" x 61 ½" rectangles	Fabric I

Finished Size:
51 ½" x 51 ½"

Recipe

Sew four Silo Barn Blocks from page 80.

Sashing Blocks:

Assemble two Fabric A rectangles and one Fabric E rectangle.

Sashing Block should measure 3 ½" x 14 ½".

Make twelve.

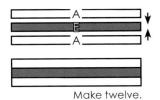

Make twelve.

Nine Patch Blocks:

Assemble five matching Fabric F squares and four Fabric B squares.

Nine Patch Block should measure 3 ½" x 3 ½".

Make nine.

Make nine.

Quilt Center:

Assemble the Quilt Center.

Press toward the Sashing Blocks.

Quilt Center should measure 37 ½" x 37 ½".

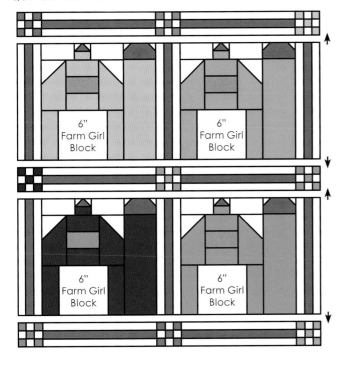

Borders:

Attach side inner borders using the Fabric C strips.

Attach top and bottom inner borders using the Fabric D strips.

Piece the Fabric G strips end to end.

Subcut into:

    2 - 6 ½" x 39 ½" strips (G1)

    2 - 6 ½" x 51 ½" strips (G2)

Attach side outer borders using the Fabric G1 strips.

Attach top and bottom outer borders using the Fabric G2 strips.

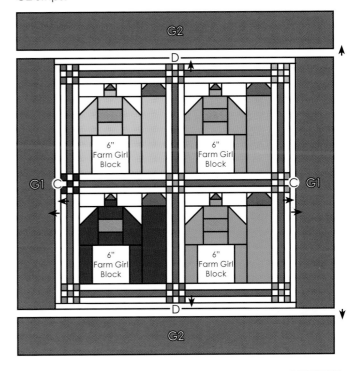

Finishing:

Piece the Fabric H strips end to end for binding.

Piece the Fabric I rectangles together with a ½" seam for a horizontal or vertical backing.

Press open for less bulk.

Quilt and bind as desired.

Silo Barn Tablerunner

Cutting Instructions:

Background (½ yard):
- Cut 4   2 ½" x 18 ½" rectangles   Fabric A
- Cut 4   2 ½" x 14 ½" rectangles   Fabric B

Patchwork (scraps):
- Cut 36   3 ½" squares   Fabric C

Binding (½ yard):
- Cut 5   2 ½" x width of fabric strips   Fabric D

Backing (1 ⅞ yards):
- Cut 1   28 ½" x 64 ½" rectangle   Fabric E

Finished Size:
18 ½" x 54 ½"

Recipe

Sew two Silo Barn Blocks from page 80.

Patchwork Block:

Assemble thirty-six Fabric C squares.

Press rows in alternating directions.

Patchwork Block should measure 18 ½" x 18 ½".

Make one.

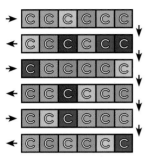
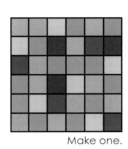

Make one.

Framed Silo Barn Blocks:

Assemble two Fabric B rectangles, one Silo Barn Block and two Fabric A rectangles.

Framed Silo Barn Block should measure 18 ½" x 18 ½".

Make two.

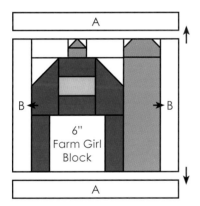

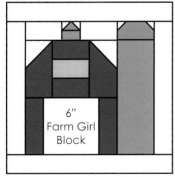

Make two.

Tablerunner Center:

Assemble the Tablerunner Center.

Tablerunner Center should measure 18 ½" x 54 ½".

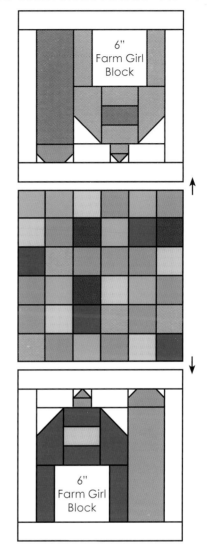

Finishing:

Piece the Fabric D strips end to end for binding.

Quilt and bind as desired.

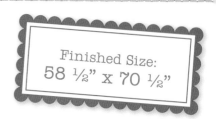

Finished Size:
58 ½" x 70 ½"

Cutting Instructions:

Background and Border (4 ⅜ yards):

- Cut 166	5" squares	Fabric A
- Cut 8	3 ½" x width of fabric strips	Fabric B
- Cut 4	2 ½" x 24 ½" rectangles	Fabric C
- Cut 2	1 ½" x 20 ½" rectangles	Fabric D
- Cut 2	1 ½" x 18 ½" rectangles	Fabric E

Pinwheels (scraps):

- Cut 166	5" squares	Fabric F

Tractor Border (⅓ yard):

- Cut 2	1 ½" x 22 ½" rectangles	Fabric G
- Cut 2	1 ½" x 20 ½" rectangles	Fabric H

Binding (¾ yard):

- Cut 8	2 ½" x width of fabric strips	Fabric I

½" Yellow Ric Rac (8 yards):

- Cut 2	63 ½" pieces	Fabric J
- Cut 2	75 ½" pieces	Fabric K

Backing (4 ½ yards):

- Cut 2	34 ¾" x 80 ½" rectangles	Fabric L

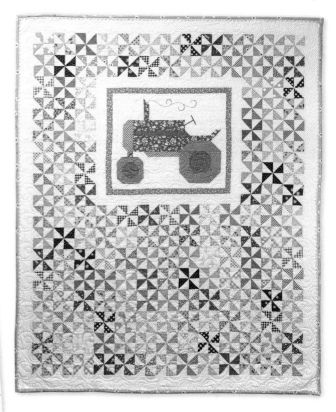

Recipe

Sew one Tractor Block from page 82.

Pinwheel Blocks:

Draw a diagonal line twice on the wrong side of the Fabric A squares.

Make one hundred sixty-six.

Make one hundred sixty-six.

With right sides facing, layer a Fabric A square with a Fabric F square.

Stitch on the drawn lines.

Make one hundred sixty-six Partial Fabric A/F Units.

Make one hundred sixty-six.

Cut the Partial Fabric A/F Units into quarters.

Fabric A/F Unit should measure 2 ½" x 2 ½".

Make six hundred sixty-four.

Make six hundred sixty-four.

Trim ¼" away from the seam.

Half Square Triangle Unit should measure 2 ½" x 2 ½".

Make six hundred sixty-four.

Make six hundred sixty-four.

Assemble four matching Half Square Triangle Units.

Pinwheel Block should measure 4 ½" x 4 ½".

Make one hundred sixty-six.

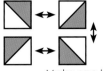

Make one hundred sixty-six.

Plow Day Block:

Assemble two Fabric D rectangles, the Tractor Block and two Fabric E rectangles.

Framed Plow Day Unit should measure 18 ½" x 22 ½".

Make one.

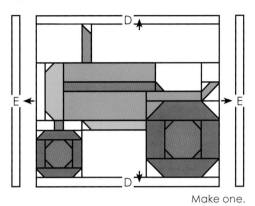

Make one.

Assemble two Fabric G rectangles, the Framed Plow Day Unit and two Fabric H rectangles.

Bordered Plow Day Unit should measure 20 ½" x 24 ½".

Make one.

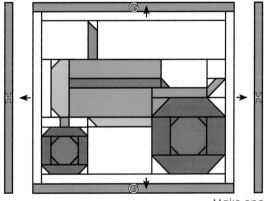

Make one.

Plow Day Quilt

Assemble the Plow Day Block.
Plow Day Block should measure 24 ½" x 28 ½".
Make one.

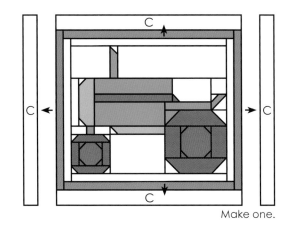

Make one.

Quilt Rows:

Assemble thirteen Pinwheel Blocks.
Long Pinwheel Row should measure 4 ½" x 52 ½".
Make ten.

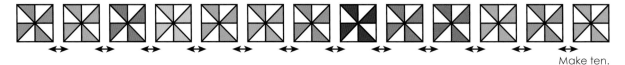

Make ten.

Assemble six Pinwheel Blocks.
Short Pinwheel Row should measure 4 ½" x 24 ½".
Make six.

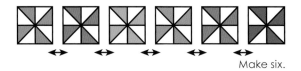

Make six.

Assemble six Short Pinwheel Rows and the Plow Day Block.
Tractor Row should measure 24 ½" x 52 ½".
Make one.

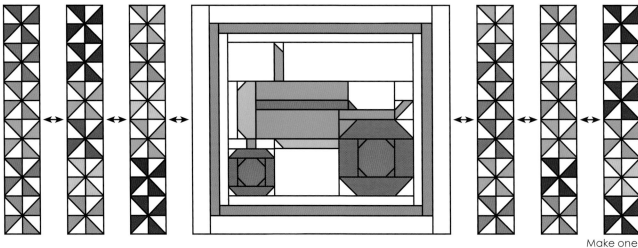

Make one.

Quilt Center:

Assemble the Quilt Center.

Quilt Center should measure 52 ½" x 64 ½".

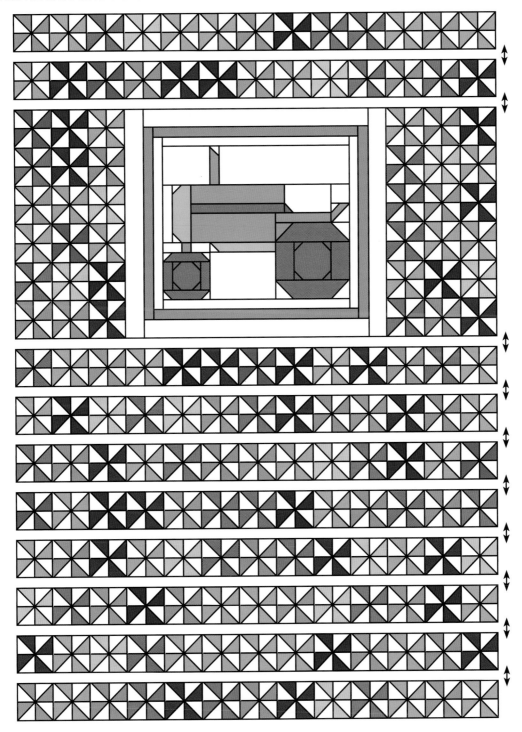

Plow Day Quilt

Borders:

Piece the Fabric B strips end to end.

Subcut into:

      2 - 3 ½" x 64 ½" strips (B1)

      2 - 3 ½" x 58 ½" strips (B2)

Attach side borders using the Fabric B1 strips.

Attach top and bottom borders using the Fabric B2 strips.

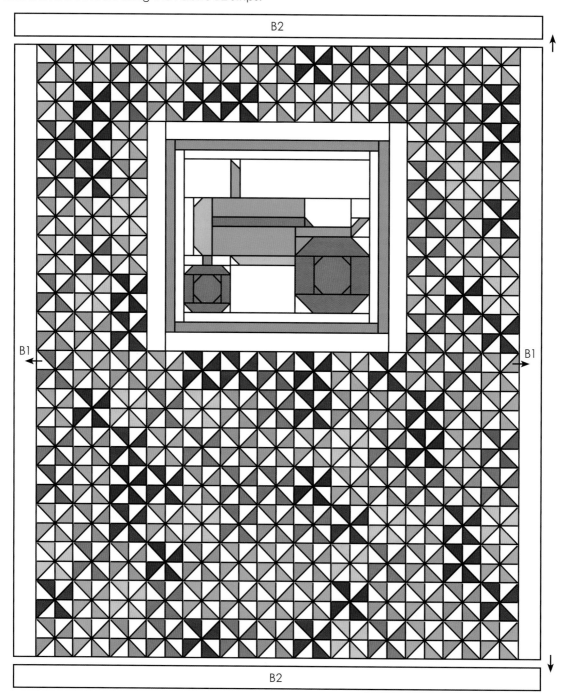

Finishing:

Attach the Fabric J ric rac pieces to the top and bottom of the quilt.

Attach the Fabric K ric rac pieces to the sides of the quilt.

Clip the ric rac at the end of each row so the unfinished ends are even with the outside edge of the quilt and will be enclosed in the binding. Use Fray Check on the ends to prevent fraying.

Piece the Fabric I strips end to end for binding.

Piece the Fabric L rectangles together with a ½" seam for a vertical backing. Press open for less bulk.

Quilt and bind as desired.

Mix & Match
Setting Quilts

Make all of these quilts multiple times! Choose a single Farm Girl Block to shine,
but don't forget to try other blocks for equally amazing and
unique results.

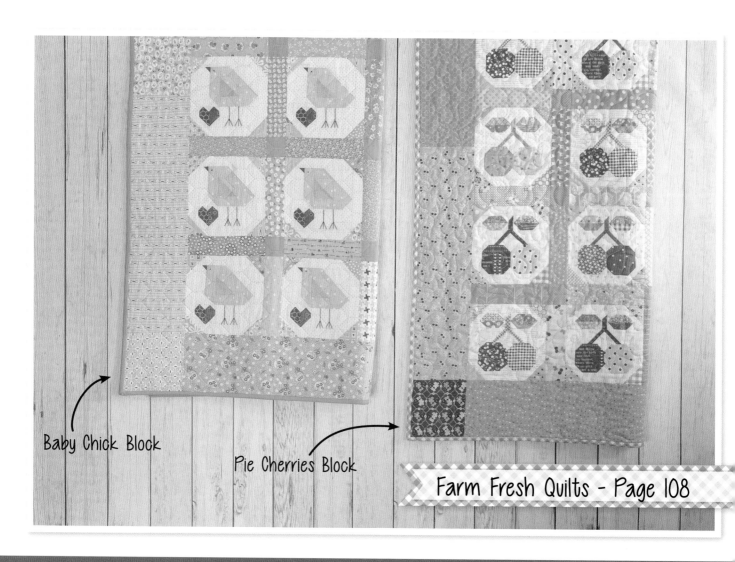

Baby Chick Block

Pie Cherries Block

Farm Fresh Quilts - Page 108

Small County Fair Quilts - Page 112

Spring Star Block

Milking Day Block

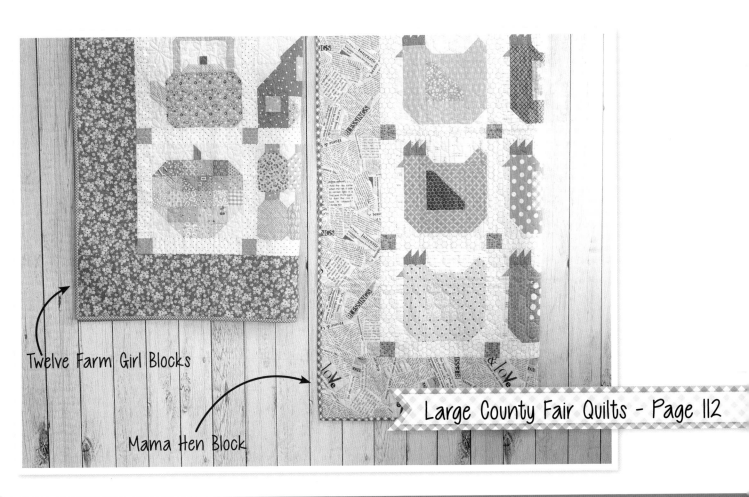

Twelve Farm Girl Blocks

Mama Hen Block

Large County Fair Quilts - Page 112

Picnic Quilts - Page 114

Scrappy Maple Leaf Block

Simple Star Block

Square Dance Quilts - Page 118

Feed and Seed Block

Sixteen Simple Star Blocks & Nine Farm Girl Blocks

Farm Kitchen Potholders - Page 120

As you can see with the Farm Kitchen Potholders - the possibilities are endless!

Butter Churn Block

Sunny Sunflower Block

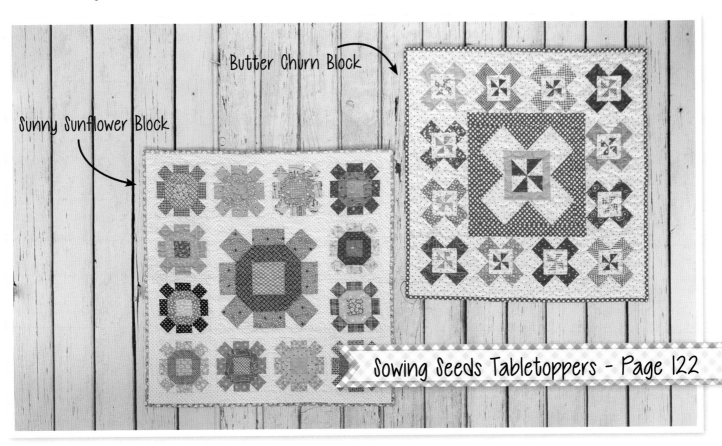

Sowing Seeds Tabletoppers - Page 122

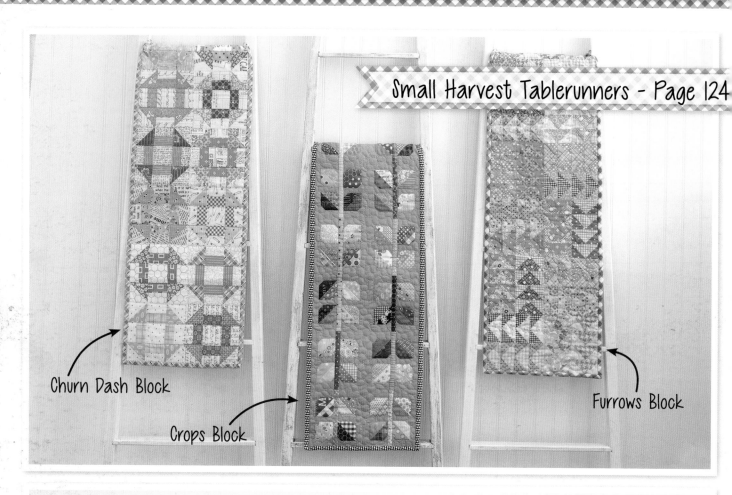

Small Harvest Tablerunners - Page 124

Churn Dash Block

Crops Block

Furrows Block

Large Harvest Tablerunners - Page 124

Tumbleweed Block

Apron Strings Block

Gingham Block

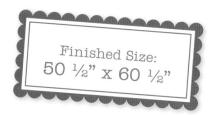

Finished Size:
50 ½" x 60 ½"

Cutting Instructions:

Background (⅞ yard):
- Cut 40   1 ½" x 8 ½" rectangles   Fabric A
- Cut 40   1 ½" x 6 ½" rectangles   Fabric B

Block Corners and Sashing (scraps):
- Cut 31   2 ½" x 8 ½" rectangles   Fabric C
- Cut 80   2 ½" squares   Fabric D

Cornerstones (scraps):
- Cut 12   2 ½" squares   Fabric E

Border (eight ⅓ yards):
- Cut 4   6 ½" x 24 ½" rectangles   Fabric F
- Cut 4   6 ½" x 19 ½" rectangles   Fabric G

Border Corners (scraps):
- Cut 4   6 ½" squares   Fabric H

Binding (⅝ yard):
- Cut 7   2 ½" x width of fabric strips   Fabric I

Backing (3 ⅜ yards):
- Cut 2   35 ¾" x 60 ½" rectangles   Fabric J

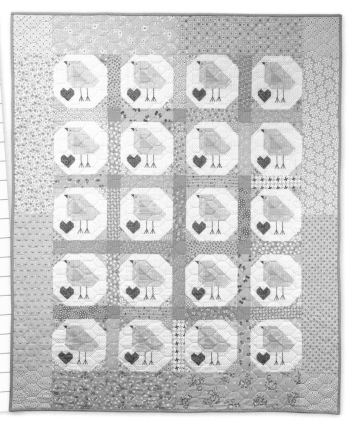

Recipe

Sew twenty 6" Farm Girl Blocks. This quilt features the Baby Chick Block from page 10.

Farm Fresh Blocks:

Assemble two Fabric B rectangles, one 6" Farm Girl Block and two Fabric A rectangles.

Partial Farm Fresh Unit should measure 8 ½" x 8 ½".

Make twenty.

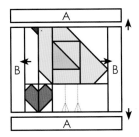 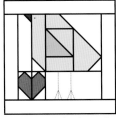

Make twenty.

Draw a diagonal line on the wrong side of the Fabric D squares.

With right sides facing, layer a Fabric D square on one corner of a Partial Farm Fresh Unit.

Stitch on the drawn line and trim ¼" away from the seam.

Make twenty.

Repeat on the remaining corners of the Partial Farm Fresh Unit.

Farm Fresh Block should measure 8 ½" x 8 ½".

Make twenty.

Make twenty.

Farm Fresh Quilt Setting

Quilt Center:

Assemble the Quilt Center.

Use the Fabric C rectangles for sashing and the Fabric E squares for cornerstones. Press toward the sashing.

Quilt Center should measure 38 ½" x 48 ½".

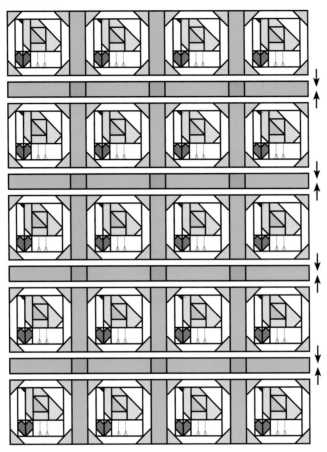

Borders:

Assemble two Fabric F rectangles.

Side Border should measure 6 ½" x 48 ½".

Make two.

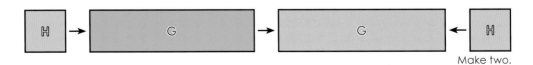

Make two.

Assemble two Fabric H squares and two Fabric G rectangles.

Top and Bottom Border should measure 6 ½" x 50 ½".

Make two.

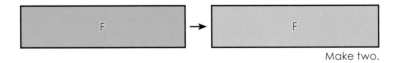

Make two.

Attach Side Borders.
Attach Top and Bottom Borders.

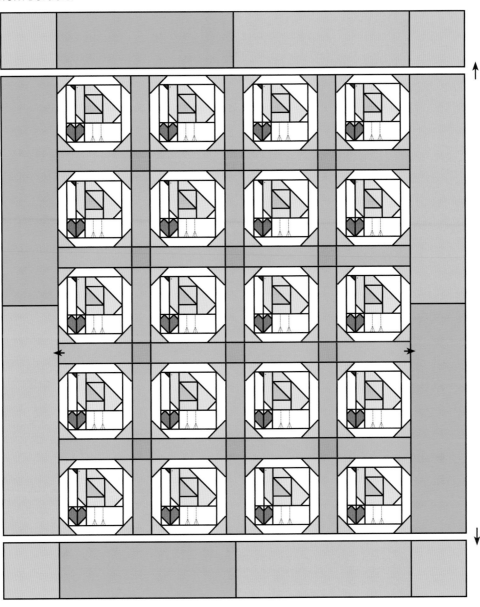

Finishing:

Piece the Fabric I strips end to end for binding.

Piece the Fabric J rectangles together with a ½" seam for a horizontal backing.
Press open for less bulk.

Quilt and bind as desired.

County Fair Quilt Setting

Small Version Cutting Instructions:

Sashing (½ yard):
- Cut 31   1 ½" x 6 ½" rectangles   Fabric A

Cornerstones (⅛ yard):
- Cut 20   1 ½" squares   Fabric B

Border (four ¼ yards):
- Cut 1   4 ½" x width of fabric strip (four total) Fabric C

Binding (½ yard):
- Cut 5   2 ½" x width of fabric strips   Fabric D

Backing (1 ⅓ yards):
- Cut 1   40 ½" x 47 ½" rectangle   Fabric E

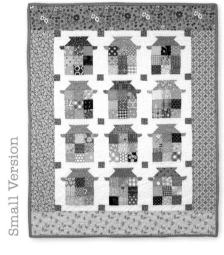

Finished Size: 30 ½" x 37 ½"

Small Version

Recipe

This small version features twelve 6" Milking Day Blocks from page 45.

This large version features twelve 12" Mama Hen Blocks from page 42.

Finished Size: 60 ½" x 74 ½"

Large Version Cutting Instructions:

Sashing (⅞ yard):
- Cut 31   2 ½" x 12 ½" rectangles   Fabric A

Cornerstones (⅓ yard):
- Cut 20   2 ½" squares   Fabric B

Border (1 ⅞ yards):
- Cut 7   8 ½" x width of fabric strips   Fabric C

Binding (¾ yard):
- Cut 8   2 ½" x width of fabric strips   Fabric D

Backing (4 ¾ yards):
- Cut 2   35 ¾" x 84 ½" rectangles   Fabric E

Large Version

Quilt Center:

Assemble the Quilt Center.

Use the Fabric A rectangles for sashing and the Fabric B squares for cornerstones. Press toward the sashing.

Quilt Center should measure 22 ½" x 29 ½" (44 ½" x 58 ½").

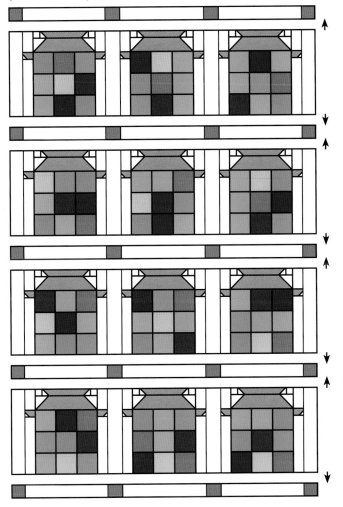

Borders:

Small version -
Subcut the Fabric C strips into:

        2 - 4 ½" x 29 ½" strips (C1 - small version)
        2 - 4 ½" x 30 ½" strips (C2 - small version)

Large version -
Piece the Fabric C strips end to end. Subcut the Fabric C strips into:

        2 - 8 ½" x 58 ½" strips (C1 - large version)
        2 - 8 ½" x 60 ½" strips (C2 - large version)

Attach side borders using the Fabric C1 strips.

Attach top and bottom borders using the Fabric C2 strips.

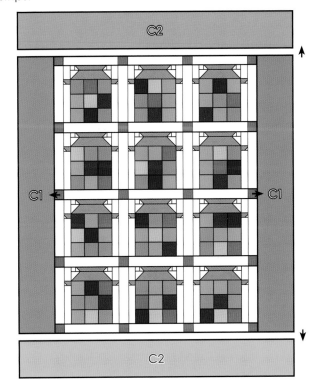

Finishing:

Piece the Fabric D strips end to end for binding.

For the large version, piece the Fabric E rectangles together with a ½" seam for a vertical backing.

Press open for less bulk.

Quilt and bind as desired.

Picnic Quilt Setting

Cutting Instructions:

Border (1 yard):
- Cut 8   3 ½" x width of fabric strips   Fabric A

Binding (¾ yard):
- Cut 8   2 ½" x width of fabric strips   Fabric B

Backing (4 ¼ yards):
- Cut 2   38 ¾" x 76 ½" rectangles   Fabric C

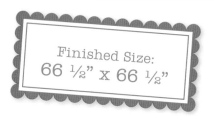

Finished Size:
66 ½" x 66 ½"

Recipe

Sew thirty-six 6" Farm Girl Blocks and sixteen 12" Farm Girl Blocks. This quilt features the Simple Star Block from page 61.

Picnic Blocks:

Assemble two 6" Farm Girl Blocks and one 12" Farm Girl Block.

Picnic One Unit should measure 12 ½" x 18 ½".

Make sixteen.

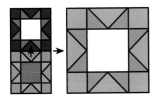 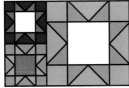

Make sixteen.

Assemble one 6" Farm Girl Block and one Picnic One Unit.

Start stitching ¼" away from the left. Backstitch.

Make four Picnic Two Units.

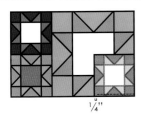 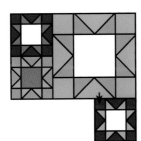

¼"

Make four.

Assemble one Picnic Two Unit and one Picnic One Unit.

Make four Picnic Three Units.

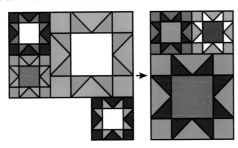

Make four.

Assemble one Picnic Three Unit and one Picnic One Unit.

Make four Picnic Four Units.

Make four.

Picnic Quilt Setting

Assemble the Picnic Block.

Picnic Block should measure 30 ½" x 30 ½".

Make four.

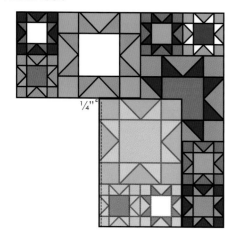

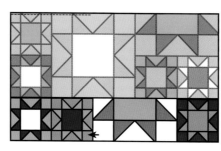

Make four.

Quilt Center:

Assemble the Quilt Center.

Quilt Center should measure 60 ½" x 60 ½".

Borders:

Piece the Fabric A strips end to end.

Subcut into:

    2 - 3 ½" x 60 ½" strips (A1)
    2 - 3 ½" x 66 ½" strips (A2)

Attach side borders using the Fabric A1 strips.

Attach top and bottom borders using the Fabric A2 strips.

Finishing:

Piece the Fabric B strips end to end for binding.

Piece the Fabric C rectangles together with a ½" seam for a horizontal or vertical backing.

Press open for less bulk.

Quilt and bind as desired.

Cutting Instructions:

Sashing (1 ⅝ yards):
- Cut 24   6 ½" x 12 ½" rectangles   Fabric A

Border (1 ¼ yards):
- Cut 8   4 ½" x width of fabric strips   Fabric B

Binding (¾ yard):
- Cut 8   2 ½" x width of fabric strips   Fabric C

Backing (4 ⅜ yards):
- Cut 2   39 ¾" x 78 ½" rectangles   Fabric D

Finished Size:
68 ½" x 68 ½"

Recipe

Sew sixteen 6" Farm Girl Blocks and nine 12" Farm Girl Blocks. This quilt features the Simple Star Block from page 61 and nine different 12" Farm Girl Blocks.

Square Dance Quilt Setting

Quilt Center:

Assemble the Quilt Center.

Use the Fabric A rectangles for sashing. Press toward the sashing.

Quilt Center should measure 60 ½" x 60 ½".

Borders:

Piece the Fabric B strips end to end.

Subcut into:

> 2 - 4 ½" x 60 ½" strips (B1)
>
> 2 - 4 ½" x 68 ½" strips (B2)

Attach side borders using the Fabric B1 strips.

Attach top and bottom borders using the Fabric B2 strips.

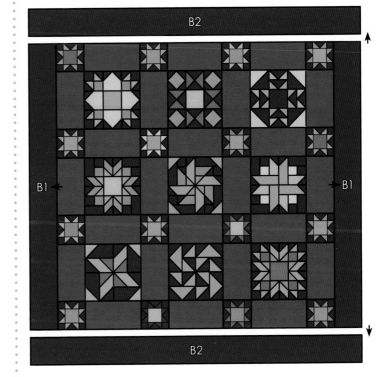

Finishing:

Piece the Fabric C strips end to end for binding.

Piece the Fabric D rectangles together with a ½" seam for a horizontal or vertical backing.

Press open for less bulk.

Quilt and bind as desired.

Cutting Instructions:

Border (⅛ yard):
- Cut 2   1 ½" x 8 ½" rectangles   Fabric A
- Cut 2   1 ½" x 6 ½" rectangles   Fabric B

Binding (⅛ yard):
- Cut 1   2 ½" x width of fabric strip   Fabric C

Insul-Bright (scrap):
- Cut 1   10" square   Fabric D

Backing (scrap):
- Cut 1   10" square   Fabric E

Finished Size:
8 ½" x 8 ½"

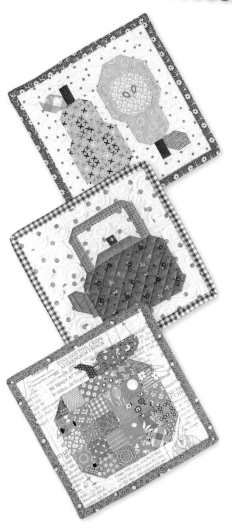

Recipe

Sew one 6" Farm Girl Block. These potholders feature the Fresh Pears Block from page 32, the Kettle's On! Block from page 39 and the Patchwork Pumpkin Block from page 51.

Potholder Top:

Assemble two Fabric B rectangles, the 6" Farm Girl Block and two Fabric A rectangles.

Potholder Top should measure 8 ½" x 8 ½".

Make one.

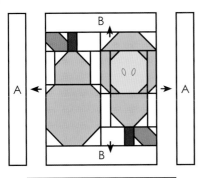

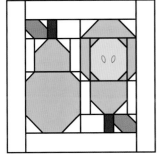

Make one.

Finishing:

Layer the Potholder Top (face up), the Fabric D Insul-Bright and the Fabric E Backing (face down).

Baste ⅛" around the inside of the Potholder Top.

Trim excess Insul-Bright and Backing.

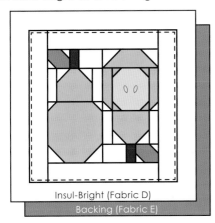

Insul-Bright (Fabric D)

Backing (Fabric E)

Quilt and bind as desired.

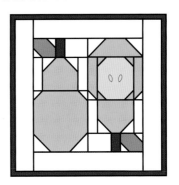

Cutting Instructions:

Sashing and Border (¾ yard):

- Cut 2	2" x 15 ½" rectangles	Fabric A
- Cut 2	2" x 12 ½" rectangles	Fabric B
- Cut 12	1 ½" x 6 ½" rectangles	Fabric C
- Cut 2	2" x 30 ½" strips	Fabric D
- Cut 2	2" x 27 ½" strips	Fabric E

Binding (½ yard):

- Cut 4	2 ½" x width of fabric strips	Fabric F

Backing (1 ⅛ yards):

- Cut 1	40 ½" square	Fabric G

Finished Size:
30 ½" x 30 ½"

Recipe

Sew twelve 6" Farm Girl Blocks and one 12" Farm Girl Block. This quilt features the Sunny Sunflower Block from page 66.

Sowing Seeds Block:

Assemble two Fabric B rectangles, the 12" Farm Girl Block and two Fabric A rectangles.

Sowing Seeds Block should measure 15 ½" x 15 ½".

Make one.

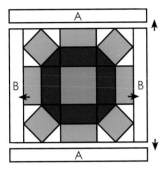
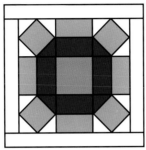

Make one.

Sowing Seeds Rows:

Assemble four 6" Farm Girl Blocks and three Fabric C rectangles.

Long Sowing Seeds Row should measure 6 ½" x 27 ½".

Make two.

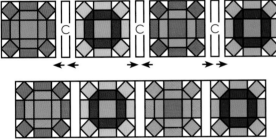

Make two.

Assemble three Fabric C rectangles and two 6" Farm Girl Blocks.

Short Sowing Seeds Row should measure 6 ½" x 15 ½".

Make two.

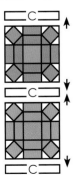
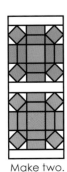

Make two.

Quilt Center:

Assemble the Quilt Center.

Quilt Center should measure 27 ½" x 27 ½".

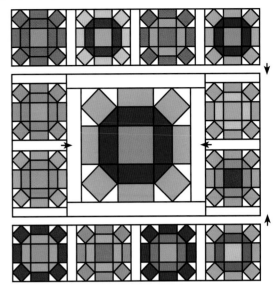

Borders:

Attach side borders using the Fabric E strips.

Attach top and bottom borders using the Fabric D strips.

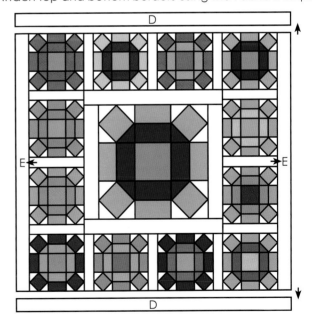

Finishing:

Piece the Fabric F strips end to end for binding.

Quilt and bind as desired.

Small Version Cutting Instructions:

Binding (½ yard):
- Cut 4   2 ½" x width of fabric strips   Fabric A

Backing (1 ⅓ yards):
- Cut 1   22 ½" x 46 ½" rectangle   Fabric B

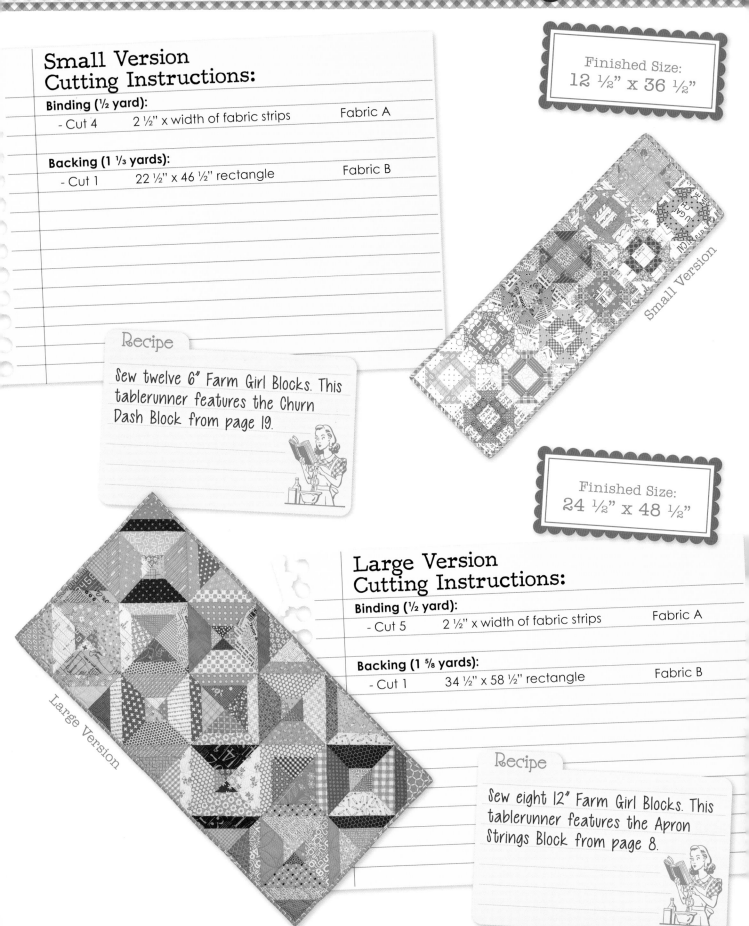

Small Version

Recipe

Sew twelve 6" Farm Girl Blocks. This tablerunner features the Churn Dash Block from page 19.

Large Version

Large Version Cutting Instructions:

Binding (½ yard):
- Cut 5   2 ½" x width of fabric strips   Fabric A

Backing (1 ⅝ yards):
- Cut 1   34 ½" x 58 ½" rectangle   Fabric B

Recipe

Sew eight 12" Farm Girl Blocks. This tablerunner features the Apron Strings Block from page 8.

Small Tablerunner Center:

Assemble the Small Tablerunner Center.

Small Tablerunner Center should measure 12 ½" x 36 ½".

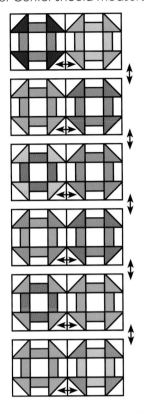

Large Tablerunner Center:

Assemble the Large Tablerunner Center.

Large Tablerunner Center should measure 24 ½" x 48 ½".

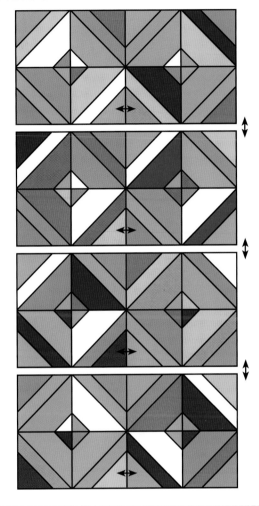

Small Tablerunner Finishing:

Piece the Fabric A strips end to end for binding.

Quilt and bind as desired.

Large Tablerunner Finishing:

Piece the Fabric A strips end to end for binding.

Quilt and bind as desired.

More Farm Girl Quilts

Sampler quilts make my quilty heart sing! Assemble a multitude of my Farm Girl Blocks, as many as you please, into any of these three Farm Girl Quilts.

Cutting Instructions:

Background and Borders (1 ⅜ yards):

- Cut 12	2 ½" x 3" rectangles	Fabric A
- Cut 12	2" x 3 ½" rectangles	Fabric B
- Cut 24	1 ¾" squares	Fabric C
- Cut 6	1 ½" x 6 ½" rectangles	Fabric D
- Cut 12	1 ½" x 4 ½" rectangles	Fabric E
- Cut 12	1 ½" x 3" rectangles	Fabric F
- Cut 24	1 ½" squares	Fabric G
- Cut 17	1 ½" x width of fabric strips	Fabric H

Trees (scraps):

- Cut 6	4 ½" squares	Fabric I
- Cut 6	3 ½" squares	Fabric J
- Cut 6	1 ½" x 6 ½" rectangles	Fabric K

Tree Trunks (scraps):

- Cut 6	1 ½" x 2 ½" rectangles	Fabric L
- Cut 6	1 ½" squares	Fabric M

Second Border (½ yard):

- Cut 7	1 ½" x width of fabric strips	Fabric N

Fourth Border (2 ⅛ yards):

- Cut 2	6 ½" x 58 ½" length of fabric strips	Fabric O
- Cut 2	6 ½" x 66 ½" length of fabric strips	Fabric P

Binding (¾ yard):

- Cut 8	2 ½" x width of fabric strips	Fabric Q

Backing (4 ½ yards):

- Cut 2	38 ¾" x 80 ½" rectangles	Fabric R

Finished Size:
66 ½" x 70 ½"

Recipe

Sew sixteen 6" Farm Girl Blocks and nine 12" Farm Girl Blocks. This quilt features the Welcome Block from page 70 and the Farmhouse Block from page 27.

Tree Blocks:

Draw a diagonal line on the wrong side of the Fabric G squares.

With right sides facing, layer a Fabric G square on one corner of a Fabric J square.

Stitch on the drawn line and trim ¼" away from the seam.

Make six.

Repeat on the remaining corners of the Fabric J square.

Small Tree Unit should measure 3 ½" x 3 ½".

Make six.

Make six.

Assemble two Fabric B rectangles and one Small Tree Unit.

Top Tree Unit should measure 3 ½" x 6 ½".

Make six.

Make six.

Draw a diagonal line on the wrong side of the Fabric C squares.

With right sides facing, layer a Fabric C square on one corner of a Fabric I square.

Stitch on the drawn line and trim ¼" away from the seam.

Make six.

Repeat on the remaining corners of the Fabric I square.

Large Tree Unit should measure 4 ½" x 4 ½".

Make six.

Make six.

Assemble two Fabric E rectangles and one Large Tree Unit.

Bottom Tree Unit should measure 4 ½" x 6 ½".

Make six.

Make six.

Assemble two Fabric F rectangles and one Fabric M square.

Top Tree Trunk Unit should measure 1 ½" x 6 ½".

Make six.

Make six.

Assemble two Fabric A rectangles and one Fabric L rectangle.

Bottom Tree Trunk Unit should measure 2 ½" x 6 ½".

Make six.

Make six.

Assemble the Tree Block.

Tree Block should measure 6 ½" x 12 ½".

Make six.

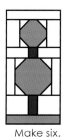 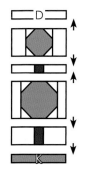

Make six.

Farmhouse Lane Quilt

Quilt Center:

Piece the 1 ½" Fabric H strips end to end.

Subcut into:

      6 - 1 ½" x 48 ½" strips (H1)

      2 - 1 ½" x 54 ½" strips (H2)

      2 - 1 ½" x 56 ½" strips (H3)

      2 - 1 ½" x 54 ½" strips (H4)

Assemble the Quilt Center.

When joining blocks press seams open.

Quilt Center should measure 48 ½" x 54 ½".

Borders:

Piece the 1 ½" Fabric N strips end to end.
Subcut into:

      2 - 1 ½" x 50 ½" strips (N1)
      2 - 1 ½" x 56 ½" strips (N2)

Attach side first borders using the Fabric H2 strips.

Attach top and bottom second borders using the Fabric N1 strips. Attach side second borders using the Fabric N2 strips.

Attach side third borders using the Fabric H3 strips. Attach top and bottom third borders using the Fabric H4 strips.

Attach side fourth borders using the Fabric O strips. Attach top and bottom fourth borders using the Fabric P strips.

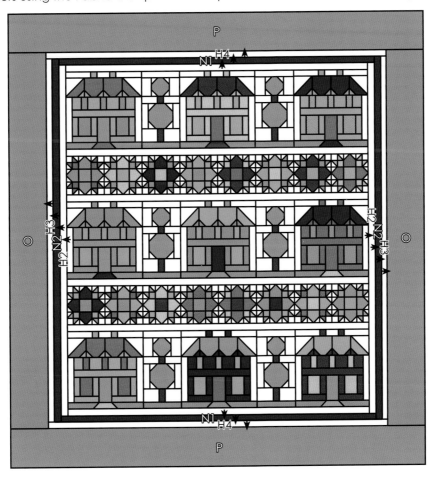

Finishing:

Piece the Fabric Q strips end to end for binding.

Piece the Fabric R rectangles together with a ½" seam for a vertical backing.
Press open for less bulk.

Quilt and bind as desired.

Scrappy Haystack Sampler Quilt

Finished Size:
92 ½" x 92 ½"

Cutting Instructions:

Sashing (1 ⅞ yards):
- Cut 112   1 ½" x 12 ½" rectangles   Fabric A

Cornerstones (scraps):
- Cut 64   1 ½" squares   Fabric B

Binding (1 yard):
- Cut 11   2 ½" x width of fabric strips   Fabric C

Backing (8 ⅝ yards):
- Cut 3   34 ¾" x 102 ½" rectangles   Fabric D

Recipe

Sew thirteen different 12" Farm Girl Blocks and one hundred forty-four 6" Haystack Blocks from page 38.

Scrappy Haystack Blocks:

Assemble four Haystack Blocks.
Scrappy Haystack Block should measure 12 ½" x 12 ½".
Make thirty-six.

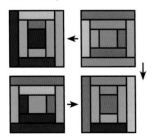

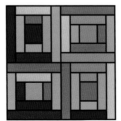

Make thirty-six.

Scrappy Haystack Sampler Quilt

Quilt Center:

Assemble the Quilt Center.

Use the Fabric A rectangles for sashing and the Fabric B squares for cornerstones. Press toward the sashing.

Quilt Center should measure 92 ½" x 92 ½".

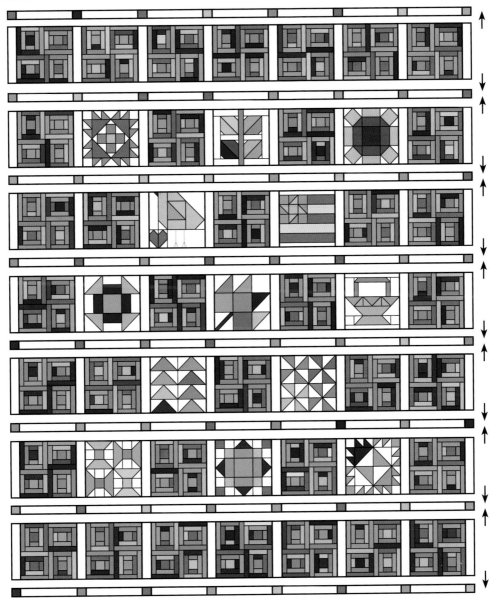

Finishing:

Piece the Fabric C strips end to end for binding.

Piece the Fabric D rectangles together with a ½" seam for a horizontal or vertical backing.

Press open for less bulk.

Quilt and bind as desired.

Farm Girl Sampler Quilt

Finished Size:
62 ½" x 76 ½"

Cutting Instructions:

Sashing and Borders (2 ¼ yards):

- Cut 110	1 ½" x 6 ½" rectangles	Fabric A
- Cut 6	2" x width of fabric strips	Fabric B
- Cut 212	1 ½" squares	Fabric C
- Cut 4	1 ½" squares	Fabric D
- Cut 7	1 ½" x width of fabric strips	Fabric E

Cornerstones (scraps):

- Cut 63	1 ½" squares	Fabric F

Second Border (½ yard):

- Cut 106	1 ½" x 2 ½" rectangles	Fabric G

Fourth Border (1 ⅔ yards):

- Cut 8	6 ½" x width of fabric strips	Fabric H

Binding (¾ yard):

- Cut 8	2 ½" x width of fabric strips	Fabric I

Backing (4 ⅞ yards):

- Cut 2	36 ¾" x 86 ½" rectangles	Fabric J

Recipe

Sew one of each 6" Farm Girl Block from pages 8 to 74 and three additional 6" Simple Star Blocks from page 61 for the corners.

Quilt Center:

Assemble the Quilt Center.

Use the Fabric A rectangles for sashing and the Fabric F squares for cornerstones. Press toward the sashing.

Quilt Center should measure 43 ½" x 57 ½".

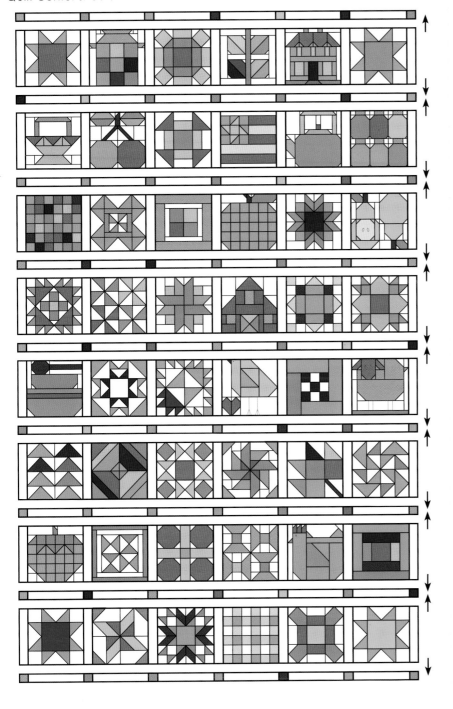

Farm Girl Sampler Quilt

Borders:

Piece the Fabric B strips end to end. Subcut into:

     2 - 2" x 57 ½" strips (B1)

     2 - 2" x 46 ½" strips (B2)

Attach side first borders using the Fabric B1 strips.

Attach top and bottom first borders using the Fabric B2 strips.

- -

Draw a diagonal line on the wrong side of the Fabric C squares.

With right sides facing, layer a Fabric C square on one end of a Fabric G rectangle.

Stitch on the drawn line and trim ¼" away from the seam.

     Make one hundred six.

Repeat on the opposite end of the Fabric G rectangle.

Flying Geese Unit should measure 1 ½" x 2 ½".

Make one hundred six.

     Make one hundred six.

- -

Assemble thirty Flying Geese Units.

Side Second Border should measure 1 ½" x 60 ½".

Make two.

     Make two.

- -

Assemble two Fabric D squares and twenty-three Flying Geese Units.

Top and Bottom Second Border should measure 1 ½" x 48 ½".

Make two.

     Make two.

- -

Attach Side Second Borders.

Attach Top and Bottom Second Borders.

- -

Piece the Fabric E strips end to end. Subcut into:

     2 - 1 ½" x 62 ½" strips (E1)

     2 - 1 ½" x 50 ½" strips (E2)

Attach side third borders using the Fabric E1 strips.

Attach top and bottom third borders using the Fabric E2 strips.

- -

Piece the Fabric H strips end to end. Subcut into:

     2 - 6 ½" x 64 ½" strips (H1)

     2 - 6 ½" x 62 ½" strips (H2)

Attach side fourth borders using the Fabric H1 strips.

Attach top and bottom fourth borders using the Fabric H2 strips.

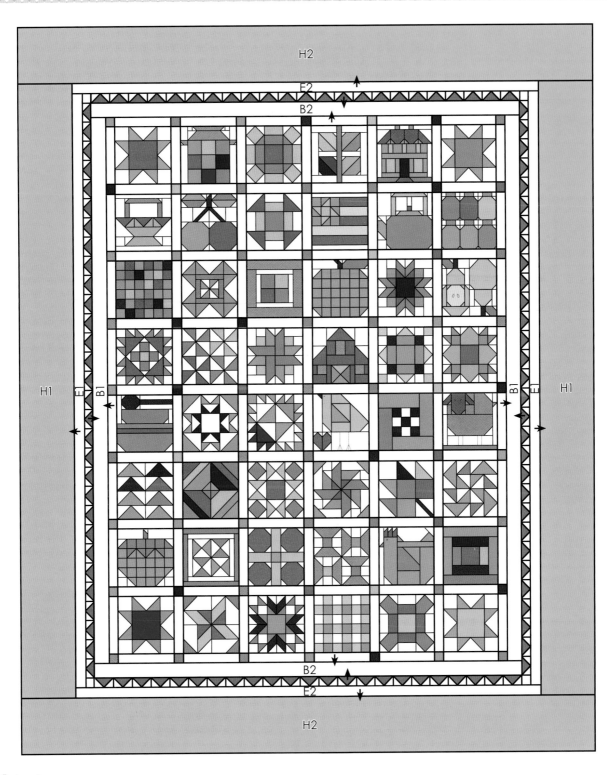

Finishing:

Piece the Fabric I strips end to end for binding.

Piece the Fabric J rectangles together with a ½" seam for a vertical backing. Press open for less bulk.

Quilt and bind as desired.